D1233250

NOTES
of a
NERVOUS
MAN

NOTES
of a
NERVOUS
MAN

James Lileks

POCKET BOOKS

New York   London   Toronto   Sydney   Tokyo   Singapore

All of the columns in this work with the exception of "White Knuckles" were previously published in the newspaper *The Saint Paul Minnesota Pioneer Press.*

POCKET BOOKS, a division of Simon & Schuster Inc. 1230 Avenue of the Americas, New York, NY 10020

Lileks, James.
   Notes of a nervous man / James Lileks.
     p. cm.
    ISBN: 0-671-73701-5 : $17.00
    I. Title.
   PS3562.I4547N68 1991
   813'.54—dc20   91-23146
                                          CIP

First Pocket Books hardcover printing November 1991

10 9 8 7 6 5 4 3 2 1

Interior design by A. P. Rosenblatt

Printed in the U.S.A.

to my loving and delightful Sara

ACKNOWLEDGMENTS

Skip this page, unless you think you might be in here, in which case I recommend skipping it anyway. *Trust* me. Unless, that is, you know you're in here, in which case read on to see who got mentioned before you did, or unless you doubt I'd ever thank you, in which case I hope to surprise you.

Thanks to:

Rich Leiby, editor of all of these pieces, savior of some, scourge of none, and, best of all, friend extraordinaire; Victoria Sloan, who first had the idea I should have a column; Deborah Howell, who thought the same thing thirteen years later. To Katherine Lanpher for that first lunch and everything afterward. To Shefchik, Morphew, and Kahn, three guys I always wanted to be for a while, just to see what it was like. To all at the *PPD* who made it a pleasure to work that side of the river, and the staff of the Cedar St. Cafe who kept me fed.

Jonathon Lazear and Jane Chelius believed in me and brought this book into the world. Hold them equally responsible, please.

My folks, of course, started this enterprise, but I owe my

vii

sister one. Kim: hope this makes you as proud of me as I am of you.

To everyone who read the *Minnesota Daily* and wondered whatever happened to me: thanks for your support back then, and now you know. And, yes, I'm just as surprised as you are.

CONTENTS

━━━━━━━━━━━━━━━━━━━━

Contents

INTRODUCTION

Don't worry, you haven't missed anything: there is no reason my name should be familiar to you. Unless you live in any of the cities whose newspapers carry my work—places such as Lumbago, Florida, or Nixon, Montana—my name means nothing.

Well, I have no idea who *you* are, either. Great relationships usually start that way, in mutual ignorance. Actually, my column is carried in Mutual Ignorance, Kansas, in the *Times-Dullard*. Maybe you've seen it. No? Okay.

Some words of introduction, then. My name—Lileks—was made up by my great-grandfather who, when pressed by Canadian immigration authorities to de-Slav his name, apparently decided to choose something that would forever be mispronounced by restaurant hostesses. We have no idea what the original name was, but I hear the possible variants each time the hostess calls for the Lelix party, the Lill-echs party, the Leeleckis party. The Leeks party. You try and look proud answering to Leeks.

It's pronounced Lie-lex, emphasis on *lie*. Not something I point out when applying for newspaper jobs.

I'm thirty-three, and, thanks to eight years of college, generally unemployable. I began as an architecture major, intending to design huge sun-obliterating towers, but quit when I learned that math was involved. I then veered like a drunk around the liberal arts curriculum, sipping from one impractical discipline after another. Every quarter I'd come home from school sporting bloodshot eyes and a T-shirt with the logo of The Throbbing Satanists or some such cretinous rock band, and tell the folks I had decided to major in Sumerian Neckwear. My father would turn several shades of gray and ochre; it was fun to watch. I ended up in English, where I spent my semesters writing awful poetry and learning to drink coffee until I vibrated like a gong.

I was rescued by journalists. I wrote an article for the school paper, and they published it. That's actually more impressive than it sounds. At most schools, I know, the college paper consists of two pinched virgins with astigmatism and a mimeograph machine. At the University of Minnesota, however, it was a big operation, turning out a daily tabloid of slanted reporting and hot-headed invective for an audience of 60,000. I ended up working there as a columnist and editor, and had so much fun I quit going to class. Never mind that I was progressing toward a degree at a rate of speed normally reserved to describe the motion of continents; I was finally learning to write.

But not news, not journalism. I wrote essays. It never occurred to me to check the want ads and note the absence of classifieds requesting "Essayist." It never struck me that a few journalism classes here and there might assist me down the road. Not for me, those pedestrian trades: I was an Essayist.

And there are plenty of jobs for Essayists. Mine was as a convenience-store clerk.

One night, a few months after I had finally left the university, twenty-five years old and unsuited for any job that did not list among its requirements an ability to explain the obscene puns in "To His Coy Mistress," I was working at Ralph and Jerry's Market, a corner store that served as a vo-tech for the local stickup artists. I was dressed in a grocer's smock, hauling a box of soda up the stairs, grimy with the dust of the stockroom, cursing the haughty little fillies from the adjacent sorority house who'd sent me down for this stuff. I sat down and wanted to weep: I had, I realized, screwed it all up. All this education, and all I was good for was schlepping sugar water up and down the stairs. Here lies one whose name is writ on Pepsi.

Victor, one of the clerks, quit that night. Decided to see what else the world promised besides selling smokes and getting held up. At closing time we went outside the store, where he threw his grocer's smock on the sidewalk, doused it with lighter fluid and burned it—the sort of gesture that seems appropriate when you are young, theatrical, and have been raiding the store's beer cooler all night long. I cheered him on, toasting his new life, feeling old and twisted and bitter, and then I pushed him into the flames.

Well, no. I just went home, smoking and slouching and frowning and smoking, wishing I had taken math classes. But—and this is the only part of my life that appears to have been scripted by Hollywood—there was a message waiting on my answering machine, a few brusque words from the editor of a local alternative weekly. He wanted me to write a piece about—what a coincidence—being a clerk in a convenience store.

That was the starting gun for what's turned out to be my adult life. I wrote for that paper, first as a food critic, then as—hallelujah!—an essayist; somewhere along the way I acquired an agent, published a novel, and was noticed by a local newspaper, which gave me the job that resulted in the collection you have now. Those years, being mostly pleasant, and hence dull, we can skip.

A few words about what follows. Most of these pieces were written under the pressure of deadlines, banged out between midnight and 3:00 A.M. the day before they were due. I've always written this way; if I'd been God and had to create the heavens and earth, I would have rested all week and waited until Sunday night, then begged an extension. When you read these pieces, think of me banging desperately away at the computer, nerves alight with caffeine, one eye on the window, dreading the appearance of daybreak, the deadline standing in the corner fondling a truncheon.

Oddly enough, given the immediacy of the job, little of this is topical—and when you're working for a newspaper, remaining untopical is no small feat. Topicality is the enemy. Somewhere out there is a writer who had the misfortune to write the funniest piece ever written on the Bicentennial, but you'll never read it; you couldn't care less about the subject matter. Cast your lot with the present, and you are yesterday's news; rummage around on the periphery of events, and you stand a chance of addressing readers in the future, through the medium of a hardcover book or, even more impressive nowadays, an audiocassette.

Here's what I mean. In 1988 I wrote a piece predicting the events of 1989—yes, there's no end to the ingenuity of us feature writers—and I posited items like the following:

"The U.S.S.R., as part of its search for better publicity, will tear down the Berlin Wall and replace it with the much more attractive Berlin Picket Fence. The first week after construction, three East Germans will be shot trying to scale the trellis. 'They were ruining the vines,' a border guard explains. 'And look at these petunias. Trampled. They'll never come back.'

"On the Democratic side, Dukakis will disappear from the national scene when an elderly man known only as Gepetto shows up, puts him in a box, and takes him home. The Democrats, stung by the latest defeat, will decide that moderate liberalism has truly been discredited and they must change their policies to recapture the electorate. The party, renamed the Hairy Stinking Wide-Eyed Bomb-Throwing Flaming Bolshevik Coalition, will field Andrei Gromyko as its next presidential candidate."

In 1989, the Soviets did indeed tear down the Wall. Andrei Gromyko died, and Dukakis fared even worse. None of this is news in 1991. That's why you see so few collections from newspaper columnists. We're all shouting at posterity, but in the wrong tongue. Posterity hasn't the faintest idea what we're talking about. Newspapers are little more than a penultimate draft of fishwrap and birdcage liner, and excelling in this medium is a sure ticket to eventual obscurity.

At least that's what I tried to tell my editors when they asked why nothing I wrote was topical, or of local interest. And, no, they didn't buy it.

There are some consolations. I was mowing the lawn the other day and inadvertently ran over the newspaper for which I worked. It was hiding under a bush, thrown there by the delivery boy, who apparently is embarrassed by the paper and feels compelled to hide it every day. The mower's blade chewed up the paper and spat out a blizzard of confetti; I had to stop mowing and rake the damn thing up. I found a scrap of paper with part of my picture on it—half my head. The balding portion, of course. It went in with the grass clippings, which in turn will go down to the local compost heap and be reduced to a soup of nutrients for one of the city's gardens. My picture may assist next year's civic petunias.

That's more in the posterity department than most columnists can expect. Or, for that matter, deserve.

St. Paul, Minnesota
September 1990

1

DOMESTIC
LIFE

In the course of two years, I became, technically, an adult.

I entered my thirties. I had thought this to be a vast, wide Rubicon, but it turned out to be something I could wade across in one night. (Actually, after the party I had to be carried.) I felt relieved to be thirty—I could still be hip, but now, in addition to despising my elders, I could be condescending about those still mired in their twenties.

I got a Real Job, meaning one with dental benefits. I had an iron-clad union contract ensuring that if I fell down an elevator shaft and was subsequently buried, I could not be fired without a series of lengthy hearings. Thus emboldened:

I bought a house. The man who arranged the financing was an old friend who, on closing day, pointed out that the word "mortgage" meant "pay until you die." When I had to sell the house a year later, it was this same friend who bought it. Whether or not this means he pays and he dies, and I am now free, clear, and immortal, I have no idea.

I got married. This was the best part. Everything was in place: maturity, job, house. All that was lacking was a kind and beautiful woman to give life flavor and color, and she came along. There was a long, agonizing wait between our first date, when I wanted to propose, and our eighty-seventh date, when I actually did, but I endured.

Faced with all this happiness, I had no choice but to write endlessly about it, and pretend other people would be interested.

How to Buy
a House

━━━━━━━━━━━━━━━━━━━━━━━

THIRTEEN YEARS OF APARTMENT-DWELLING IS ENOUGH. I've tired of having people on the other side of the wall, especially the young couple in 3A who seem to be picking up extra income by working as megaphone testers. Let's not even talk about the woman upstairs, who, from the sound of the high-velocity rhythms I hear every night, either has a thigh-blistering sex life or spends her night firing Gatling guns into pie plates. I'm getting hitched this summer, and we'll need more room anyway. That's why I went looking for a house. I wanted the peace and quiet that comes with being locked into a usurious interest rate for twenty-nine years.

Problem is, I am a bad shopper. An impulse buyer. "Comparison shopping" is, by my definition, looking for what I want at several stores, then making my purchase at the one with the coolest shopping bag. But maybe I wouldn't be impulsive with a purchase of this magnitude. After all, I would be shopping with my fiancée, a model of fiscal propriety who cannot spend money without looking like a mother whose suckling babe is being ripped from her breast. She would be my ballast.

We called a realtor named Fortuna, a chain-smoking piece

of brass who sounded like she gargled with chain mail every morning, and set off to peruse the market.

It did not go well at first. The first house on Fortuna's docket was a swine barn with siding, a rental property occupied by college students. It was a shrine to Beer. There were beer posters on the wall. Pyramids of beer cans in the windows. A thin patina of exhaled beer covered every object in the living room. The wood floor had potential, but by the time you sanded it down to the grain it would have the tensile strength of airmail paper and we would have had to get around with the aid of trapeze swings.

The kitchen showed less wear, but it looked like the samples case of a color-blind linoleum salesman—a riot of fuchsia, turquoise, peach, and spittle-flecked puce, all clashing like cymbals in the hands of an angry man. And there were deep grooves in the floor, as though the house had been for a while occupied by figure skaters.

Lighting was provided by one fluorescent light. After one minute under its harsh blare I had the urge to confess to war crimes. The light made us all look ten years older. If that was the case, it could probably spoil food in mere seconds.

The only way I would live in this house would be under a court order.

"It's a pile a sticks in need of a stiff wind, if ya know what I mean," said Fortuna. We hastened on. I felt marvelous— I had seen a house and turned it down. This was going to go well. Why, maybe, if I was really strong, *we'd never buy a house at all.*

The second house was two blocks away, and Fortuna was almost apologetic upon pointing it out.

"Lacks curb appeal, as we say," she said. This means it is ugly from a distance. I opined that it also lacked nose-pressed-right-up-to-the-stucco-appeal. First of all, the lot was bad—a barren heath on the corner. No shrubbery, no fence. I had a vision of myself sitting on the steps with a shotgun across my lap to keep the kids from cutting across. Second, it did not know what kind of house it wanted to be—it was stucco on the first floor, siding on the top, sort of a residential version of a pre-op transsexual. The upper story looked as though it had been dropped there during a twister; I expected munchkins to emerge cheering and present me with a contract for a deed.

We went in anyway.

Never mind the exterior. Within was the most exquisite little home I'd seen in all of my, what, seventeen minutes of house-hunting. I knew that we wouldn't find anything better than this. The woodwork had been completely restored and looked so fresh you expected it to sprout twigs. The kitchen was outfitted with new appliances. There was a small sun porch in which we could read the papers, have coffee, tend plants, fire salt pellets into the buttocks of youngsters cutting across the lawn. The furniture was wonderful as well—of course, I later learned that furniture was rarely included in the sale.

The stained-glass window sealed the deal. The motif of grapes and vines matched our dishes. We stood there silent, thinking the same terrifying thought: we are going to go $95,000 in debt in order to have a house that matches a $259 set of stoneware.

But the smile on my fiancée's face said it all. Sara wanted this house. Sara, who is the sort of person who comparison shops for newspapers, wanted us to buy the second house we'd seen. I saw this, and reveled; I felt that same deep satisfaction that comes when you've dragged someone else down to your level. But we had to be Careful, Cautious Shoppers. I asked Fortuna to take us to a series of progressively uglier and more expensive houses.

"No problem," she said, lighting a cigarette. "Got a million of 'em."

Briefly:

House #3. Vinyl siding. Looked as though it were made entirely out of plastic. I went around the back looking for the Mattel trademark, half expecting to find a giant hinge; surely gargantuan preteens would be along soon to open the thing up and play with us as though we were posable dolls.

House #4, or the Trompe L'Oeil House. Fake knotty-pine veneer wood inside. Wallpaper tricked up to resemble a forest glade. Mirrors on the ceiling in the bedroom. I did not like the idea of making out a check to pay for a house I was not certain was actually there.

House #5. Decorative style: wagonwheel chic. Western decor—hurricane lamps, sepia photos of droopy-eyed and probably syphilitic cowboys, signs prohibiting spitting, battered spittoons encouraging spitting. Leather chairs from the days when Texas was still an independent republic. After two rooms, we were all walking bowlegged, as though after a long ride on the trail; by the time we got to the kitchen, we expected Walter Brennan to emerge banging an iron triangle and commanding us to Come and Git It. We went and left it, instead.

House #6. The Thinnest House on Earth. You could stand in the front yard and check the condition of the stucco on both sides of the house simultaneously. Once inside, we had to crab-walk around each other. The upper floor was even thinner; we had to tour it *Great Escape*–style, sliding on our bellies on little carts. Fortuna pointed out that if we ever wanted to change neighborhoods, we could simply pick up the house and send it by surface mail.

House #7. The Clearly Someone Else's House. There was nothing wrong with this one. But it was so laden with the seller's memories that we knew we could never claim it as our own. Everywhere you looked there was a photograph, a trophy, a memento. The dining room reeked of happy family dinners, Mom in a crisp apron, Dad with the carving knife. This is, of course, preferable to picking up dad-with-the-carving-knife vibes in the stairs, the hallway, and the bathroom, and forcing the realtor to admit that the previous owner went berserk and slaughtered his family. *That's why they're a motivated seller! Legal fees!*

Nothing of this sort had happened, of course. But the sellers had put their psychic stamp on the house, and nothing short of burning it down to cinders would remove it. However we might have decided to arrange our furniture, I knew that within the year it would all be arranged just like *they* had arranged *theirs*.

"Don't you think the sofa would look better . . . over *there?*" I would say one night, not knowing why I had said it. Sara would agree, her eyes curiously blank. Five years later the walls would be full of pictures of people we didn't know. We would not notice; we would not care. When we started signing the mortgage checks with the name of the previous owner, and the bank did not complain, we'd be too far gone to notice that we had made a deal with the devil.

All that, plus the carpet was the wrong shade of blue.

"Yer absolutely right," Fortuna cawed. " 'S like someone else's grandma's house. Plus, look at the stained glass. Nothin' like your dishes, right?"

Dear Fortuna. *Helpful* Fortuna.

House #8, or the Kitchen with a Driveway. This house carried a sticker price that could be explained only if the property stood over a vast and untapped lake of oil. Once inside, we saw why it was priced so high. The house had a huge kitchen, remodeled to resemble the proportions of a small, newly independent nation. If the kitchen had been a few feet larger we could have bought the house, seceded from the Union, skipped the mortgage application and asked for foreign aid.

House #9. The Unspeakable. From the outside, it appeared to have been renovated by Mike Tyson. The sagging roof, the demolished porch, the patchy crop of beer cans and fast-food bags on the front lawn—everything suggested we would be met inside by Li'l Abner and offered a swig from a jug marked with three X's.

"Seen enough pitiful houses that are nowhere near as nice as that one you liked?" Fortuna asked. We agreed, and headed back to House #2. Its curb appeal was still deficient, but within laid the same treasures. We said we'd take it. An hour later in a pub—remember, always commit to complex, binding financial transactions over a glass of alcohol—I signed the purchase agreement and handed over a check with many zeroes.

15

"We bought a house," said Sara, stunned.

"In three hours," I said.

"That's about as fast as I've ever seen it done," said Fortuna, packing up her papers.

I paid the tab at the pub with my Visa. It has a little hologram of a bird on it. You know, if you hold the card up at a certain angle and move it back and forth, the bird appears to be moving. In the case of my card, you'd swear it's hyperventilating.

A Stranger in
Bra Country

<hr>

NEXT VALENTINE'S DAY, MEN, THIS WORD OF WARNING: Don't buy the Old Standard Gifts. If you refer to your spouse as "Old Standard," well, by all means get her something, but for the rest of you, tread carefully. Skip the chocolates and the roses; it's been done. Resist with all your might the temptation to pick her up in a rented limousine, where some prom-weary teen has recently had her virtue pawed by some sodden athlete.

Most of all, proceed with extreme caution in the lingerie department. If done right, it's the perfect gift. But if you secretly want your beloved to look like something on a tool calendar, skip it. Buying lingerie can be misery, a combination of hot-eared embarrassment and uncontrolled arousal. Just like high school.

First of all, let us be frank about the purpose of lingerie. Normally newspaper writers gets all coy when publicly discussing lingerie, as though it were everyday street clothing that, by some odd coincidence, women happened to end up wearing at home, at night. It is not normal clothing. It exists for one purpose: to be, eventually, visible for a very short time. If it is visible for a very long time—and I am trying to be delicate about this—then it is not doing its job.

17

This does not mean that lingerie has to be some lurid confection designed to fuse pacemakers and apply a cattle prod to the libido. No. Subtlety generally works best, and that's what many men fail to realize. Most men, when shopping for lingerie, tend to go for the Fifi, the French-maid-with-an-itch look. You know what I mean: the garter belts with the little hearts. The bodice with a neckline that plunges so deep you have to take a bathysphere to reach the lowermost button. The camisole in a shade of red normally found atop emergency vehicles. Anything with feathers.

This is usually not appropriate. Most women do not like overly active lingerie. This, naturally, disturbs the man; he implores his mate to try it on and walk around. Often he'll try lines like, "Come on, honey, this is the only time I get to see this without a pane of glass in the way" or "Do you know how much I spent to make you look this cheap?" to entice his helpmeet to don the clothing. At this point, the scales are likely to fall from her eyes, enabling her to see the ones on your neck. Not worth it.

Up to now, I imagine, I have earned the cheers of women and the sullen glares of men; let's reverse all that. I understand why men buy silly, obnoxious clothes for women. They are usually so intimidated by lingerie stores or departments that they grab the first thing to catch their eye and flee from the store. Women never know what men go through to buy lingerie. All you women who've ever entered a sports clothing store and purchased a jock strap, raise your hands. I thought so.

Lingerie departments are like the oceans beyond the horizons were to seafaring men of old. BEYOND HERE BE BRAS. Everything is foreign. Women's sizes, first of all, correspond to no known measurement on earth. A man's pants size is simple: waist and legs. Ditto his shirts: neck and arm. Simple and forthright.

Women have sizes like "3." And a "6," of course, is not two "3"s. There is no logic or order. When you add bra sizes, it becomes unintelligible. As I understand it, the numbers refer to actual shape, while the B, C, or D designations refer to level of education, amount of fiber in their diet, average thickness of the last four issues of *Vogue,* and the going disparity in wages.

Then there is the sight of all those bras, hanging on racks like an essay test for your imagination. It is difficult for a man—well, this man, anyway—to mosey through Bra Country without a newspaper to serve fig-leaf duty. It's worse in the stores devoted entirely to lingerie; every guy in the place has his jacket over his arm, his briefcase held high. Men, if given the choice, would walk around in these places with matador's capes held before them.

Compounding matters are the women who sell these items. They come in two varieties: young women who know exactly why you are buying them and prefer to ignore the fact for the duration of your transaction, and older women who, between the time you approach the counter and the time you leave, look more and more like a close friend of your mother.

The last time I bought foundation garments, I was helped by an older woman. It was not entirely unpleasant; there was a certain novelty in discussing my fiancée's measurements with a sixty-five-year-old stranger. But I was still on edge. I was deep into Bra Country. When I'd entered Bra Country, the women stopped and looked at me, just like in those old westerns where the piano stops playing when the stranger enters the bar. I had the impression that the good folk of Bra Country saw me as someone who came here solely to stoke his cramped and twisted libido, when in fact I wanted out as soon as possible. I found the item I wanted—SEE! IT'S NOT MY SIZE, I COULDN'T WEAR THIS IF I TRIED, IF THAT'S WHAT YOU'RE THINKING!—and took it to the substitute-teacher-pillar-of-her-church-mother-of-seven at the cash register.

"I always feel like a member of a different species every time I come to this department," I said, adding a hideous, inappropriate laugh.

She flicked a glance over the top of her glasses, a look that said, "Every time? How often *do* we come here to indulge our base and unspeakable needs?"

I fled from Bra Country and went to men's furnishings, where I was understood. (Women's underwear are "foundation garments," men's are "furnishings." Between the foundation and furnishings we have a house here.) I bought socks, a few pair of expensive, name-brand underwear that were the male equivalent of lingerie. I asked the clerk if many women came by to purchase enticing items for their menfolk.

"Awl the toime," she said in a Brooklyn accent. I asked if they seemed embarrassed, and she looked at me as though I were daft.

"It's like a duty," she said.

Obviously, then, the stigma doesn't work both ways. Men, just give her a slip for Valentine's Day. And by "slip" I mean a gift certificate signed by an official of Bra Country, confirming you had the courage to go there. Your mate will understand. Paste a sprig of lace on the slip if you're feeling romantic.

Predictable Remarks
About Plumbers

WHY IS IT ALWAYS THE WIFE WHO DISCOVERS WHEN SOME-
thing in the house breaks? My wife has discovered every
malfunction in our house. One night after we'd bought the
house, she suddenly said, "Sssh! You hear that?" I heard
nothing. "It's the upstairs toilet," she said. "It's running."

I was doubtful—partly because we were sitting around my
apartment, and had yet to move into the house. But she was
right: when we moved into the house, the upstairs commode
was fountaining away. To me it was a minor annoyance; to
her, it was a hellish cascade, and she staggered around the
house like the man in the Poe story who's convinced he hears
the beating of a dead man's heart. I fixed it.

A few weeks ago it happened again. "Sssh. Do you hear
that?" I figured that someone had left a tap running in the
retirement cottage we would buy forty years hence, but when
I listened closely I heard the sound of running water. I went
to the basement to find my water heater had burst, and my
basement looked like the boiler room of the *Titanic*. First
the toilet, now this—and after just two months of ownership.
That was it. I was taking this house back. I'd go to Dayton's,
tell them I'd bought the house from them and had lost the
receipt. At least I'd get merchandise credit.

21

Of course I did no such thing. I called a water-heater repair company that made weekend calls, and I now have a brand-new water heater guaranteed not to rust out until two months after *I* sell the house to a young, trusting couple. Fixing the toilet was just as easy, as well as nostalgic: as I lay on the bathroom floor, looking up at the commode, I was reminded of my dissolute college life.

What really confounds me, though, is that black hole, that tunnel to the stygian depths, that narrow channel of mire and despair. The sink.

Plumbers, like policemen, are never there when you need them. In a perfect world you wouldn't have to reach for a bottle of drain cleaner when your sink backs up—you'd simply go to the closet and let the plumber out. He'd be immaculately attired, clean-shaven, and would tip his hat hello when you opened the door. He would fix your drain in thirty seconds and then go back in the closet. Somewhere behind the brooms.

There are drawbacks to this—someone would have to toss a few sandwiches into the closet when you go away on vacation—but the idea is sound. This would keep you from thinking you could clean out a drain on your own. Oh, there are the everyday clogs you can dislodge, sure, the blobs of grease you can hasten on with one good jab of the plunger. But life is rarely that simple. This is how it usually works.

THE CLOG. It begins simply. You suspect nothing. After all, you pour your grease into a milk carton, and you try not to sweep coffee grounds into the sink. What you do not know is that the previous owner dined each night on a goulash consisting of concrete and roofing tar, and always flushed the leftovers down the drain.

One day the water drains, but grudgingly, taking an hour to empty the basin. When it finally drains, it emits a guttural sound, as though a cursing Slav is trapped in the pipes. The next day the drain refuses to drain at all. You now have a clog.

PLUNGING. Halfhearted plunging will not do; you have

to have the killer's instinct. You visualize the clog as a sodden hairball with bright, glinting eyes; you see it losing its grip on your pipes and swirling down screaming to a humiliating death. After a few heaves with the plunger you pull up, snarling; the drain gasps, shudders, and the water level drops. Now you are not the Slayer of Clogs but the Healer of Drains—you start to work the plunger with the grim rhythms of CPR, breathing life back into your plumbing. The water level goes down some more. You're winning.

Then you note that the water level in the other basin has risen. *That's* where the water is going. You begin to regard the clog with the same grudging respect of wartime adversaries. *He is clever, that clog. I would have done much the same.*

Do you call the plumber? Of course not! You've just begun!

BOTTLE #1. Go to the store and buy a bottle of something. Anything. Liquid drain cleaner, caustic lye, malt liquor, anything. Doesn't matter. Wait twelve hours. Wake to find water level in basin lower by the amount you'd expect to evaporate in twelve hours.

DESTROY YOUR PIPES. We have PVC pipes, plastic tubes that can be assembled by a child. (Providing that child is a member of the Pipefitter's Local, of course.) I assumed that the clog was in the trap—that's the U-shaped pipe designed by plumbers to encourage the formation of clogs. I disassembled the pipes and prepared to rout them out.

I examined the trap. My arteries should be so clean. I removed all the pipes leading into the wall: same story. The clog was IN THE WALL. If this is the case, you should either (*a*) pack up and move, or (*b*) prepare to do your dishes in a pail for the remainder of your mortgage. Or, you can continue.

THE SNAKE. You buy them at any hardware store: fifteen feet of thick coil. You shove one end into the wall and keep shoving until it hits something. After a while you'll resemble a man disposing of an unnaturally large rat.

The snake, I learned, is squeamish. Every time I gave it

a good shove it kinked up, like a soldier that had to be prodded into battle at bayonet point. After half an hour I gave up and withdrew the coil. This is where you find out how squeamish *you* are: all fifteen feet will be coated with a black viscous coagulation, the pipe's version of cholesterol. Hell, it probably *is* cholesterol.

BOTTLE #2. You're not kidding around now. Time to reach for the caustic lye. Essence of Chernobyl. Hardware stores sell it, right next to the snake. It has a big warning on the side: CAUTION—DISSOLVES SMALL CHILDREN ON CONTACT. JUST OPENING THIS BOTTLE LOWERS PROPERTY VALUES FOR A RADIUS OF SIX BLOCKS. There's also a warning about mixing the lye with other drain cleaners—an explosion may result, lifting your house into the air and dumping you on Jupiter. So you're properly terrified when you use the stuff.

I poured half the bottle into the hole in the wall. Whatever leaked out promptly dissolved the PVC gaskets. The fumes gave me a sensation equal to inhaling a fistful of hatpins. I waited for half an hour, listening for the screams of the clog. Then I reattached the pipes and ran the water.

Five minutes later, I had a sink full of caustic lye.

THE PLUMBER. The plumber always says he'll be there shortly. Do not be fooled; he operates according to something called Plumber's Time Units (PTUs). A PTU is based on Einsteinian physics—in particular, the notion that time slows as one approaches the speed of light. This explains why the plumber promises to get there as fast as he can but always takes five days to show up.

The plumber is always named Tom. He is not as impressed by your clog as you are. He even has the gall to tell you that yours is the most common kind of clog, the sort of thing that happens every ten years or so. He gets out *his* snake. It's motorized. You immediately get Snake Envy. *Well, if I had thirty feet of coil attached to a motor,* you think, *I could have taken care of it.* He atomizes the clog in five seconds, pausing only to berate you for using caustic lye.

THE LESSON. Only 0.6 percent of household malfunctions can be fixed by you, the homeowner. Ninety-nine point four percent require someone in coveralls with a beeper on his belt. In fact, everyone with a beeper is in the business of soaking money from you. My mortgage broker had a beeper. My realtor had a beeper. The man who put in the water heater had a beeper. The plumber had a beeper.

I don't know what it means, but I'll be damned if my wife gets one.

Scoop. Lift. Toss.
Scoop. Lift. Toss.

━━━━━━━━━━━━━━━━━━━━━━━━━━━━━━━━━━━━

IT'S TWICE AS MUCH FUN WHEN YOU LIVE ON A CORNER lot. Double the streets, double the view, double the sewer assessments. Best of all, double the amount of sidewalk to shovel.

I don't doubt that some of you like to shovel. Some of you put down your shovel, look hungrily at the drifts that cover your neighbor's sidewalk, and feel tempted to do their walk as well. *Just a few more feet. They won't notice.* I am not like that. I have lived in apartments for the last fourteen years; the act of shoveling is as foreign to me as turning down the thermostat. But now I have a house on a corner lot, with sidewalks so long you can stand at one end and detect the curvature of the earth. Shovel I must.

Not that I wasn't warned. When I bought the house, everyone said, "Corner lot, plenty to shovel," as though it were a piece of folk wisdom of the "red sky at night, sailor's delight" variety. I paid them no heed; in the back of my mind I figured the landlord would show up and shovel. As I am continually reminded, however, I am the landlord now. If I don't shovel, and I fall and hurt my back, I would then have to sue myself; since I am also a reasonable man, this would result in settling out of court for a lower sum.

26

When the skies dumped their ration of misery on our heads last week, I finally had to shovel. For other novices who share my situation, I have some advice to offer.

HAVE A SHOVEL HANDY. Before we joined households, my wife had a shovel, but it got lost in the move. Possibly her roommate, who moved to Arizona, took it with her. Wave a shovel at the snowbirds in Phoenix and they cringe in fear and dread and will do anything you ask. I, of course, had no shovel, so it was off to the local hardware store.

Given the trend toward pointlessly upscale merchandising, I expected to find the Digital Shovel, Precision Crafted for Maximum Displacement of Crystallized Precipitation. But shovels are still low-tech, I am happy to report. Handle, blade, and a dowel betwixt the two. They even have endearingly stupid names—one brand was called the Care Free Shovel, for those who feel compelled on occasion to throw down the shovel, spread their arms to the sky, and belt out a few bars of "Zip-a-dee-doo-dah."

The largest shovel was called the Grain Hog, and was, I imagine, designed to hurl feed at squat pink beasts with low centers of gravity. This was not an image I wanted in my head every time I stood up and hurled a load of snow onto the boulevard. One of those days, I knew, I would finally see those pigs. I would run screaming into the house, stammering about the pigs on the boulevard, and my wife would have me committed. The shovel firm would be obligated to put on a warning sticker that said WARNING! USE OF THIS SHOVEL MAY CAUSE YOU TO SEE PIGS. I didn't want any of us to go through that.

I purchased a no-name plastic shovel with a five-year guarantee. If it breaks, I'm covered. I just wrap it up, address the package to the factory in Canada, jam it down the throat of a mailbox, and wait five to ten weeks, and they send me a new shovel. By then, of course, spring will have melted all the snow, so I'm covered no matter what.

PACE YOURSELF. When I began, I was determined to do a good job, to expose every last square millimeter of

27

concrete to the cold sun. A brass band could march down my sidewalk. After a half an hour, I decided that people could damn well walk single file when they walked down my sidewalk. Half an hour later, I was shoveling out a trail best suited for unicyclists.

It bothered me that parts of the walk were left unshoveled, but I can't worry about such things. Perfection becomes an obsession if you're not careful; before you know it, you're out there taking an edge trimmer to the drifts, raking the snow and checking it with a level to make sure it's *perfectly even*. Then you lie in bed at night, listening to wind, seething and clenching your fists because the wind is ruining *everything*.

DON'T GET FANCY. There is only one way to shovel. Bend down, get a scoopful, stand up, throw it somewhere. I tried pushing the shovel along for ten feet, then throwing aside whatever accumulated. I held the handle at waist level, and ploughed down the walk. *Hey!* I thought. *This is easy!* Then I hit a slightly elevated portion of the sidewalk, driving the handle of the shovel into what football announcers calls "the groin."

I spiraled to the ground, hands over "the groin" like Adam the moment he discovered he was naked, except that I was wearing a parka. I laid there keening, and while I hate to repeat the old cliché about making a sound that only dogs can hear, dogs did arrive. All were fixed, and each bore a sympathy card in its jaws.

GIVE UP. BUY A SNOWBLOWER. Here's the real joke. I already have a snowblower. It came with the house. It is also broken. The cost to repair it certainly can't be more than, say, the cost of mailing a shovel to Canada, but I have put off repairing the beast. It's a vaguely frightening machine; decals of pointed teeth and wide, slightly insane eyes are affixed to its sides. You see machines like this in horror movies. One day it speaks to you: "Enough goddamn snow! Fetch me a newborn!" It sits in the garage, boxes piled around it.

I stopped in to the hardware store to inquire about repairs, and was immediately attracted to the new snowblowers on the showroom floor. They ranged from a pitiful Power Shovel that cost $50 and wouldn't blow the birdseed off a tile floor, to a monstrous machine that cost a grand and looked as though it should come with a sidecar.

I wanted it. First of all, it had more speeds than my car. Four forward, two reverse. ("Plus neutral!" said the salesman.) *Four speeds?* Hell, I said to the salesman, that would knock the pigs off the boulevard. He moved away.

It threw snow up to thirty feet—handy if I ever get in a feud with the folks across the street. It had a cab, a plastic cocoon that would protect me from the elements, in addition to making me look like a total idiot. It also had a headlight—insurance against those terrifying moments when you lose your way at night while snowblowing the sidewalk.

Festooning every square inch of the machine were the usual warnings directed at the criminally stupid. Just like lawn mowers bear decals pointing out that using a lawn mower to root out an ingrown hair may result in injury, so must the snowblower indemnify itself against the idiots of the world. There is the vaguely medical-sounding WARNING! DO NOT DIRECT DISCHARGE AT BYSTANDERS! or the painfully obvious WARNING! DO NOT PUT HANDS IN MOVING BLADES! Unless, of course, you want to see whether or not the blower has a range of thirty feet.

I didn't buy one. For one thing, I am not yet ready to spend a thousand dollars at a hardware store. Besides, I plan on repairing my own snowblower. It's self-propelled. Rig up some skis, and I could ride it to work.

Most important, I would never have to shovel again. Do you know that mere days after I shoveled, *it snowed again?* And I had to go out and repeat the procedure? Naturally, the cheap plastic no-name shovel broke. And of course I had ripped off the decal with the name of the company. This left me with a few options:

a) buy another cheap shovel, break it, repeat until spring;

b) buy the Grain Hog, risk madness;

c) buy the self-propelled model, explain to wife why the optional CD player was necessary;

d) steal some POLICE LINE DO NOT CROSS tape and put it across my sidewalk so people take the street;

e) set self on fire, have wife drag me up and down sidewalk.

I pursued option (*a*), of course. I bought another cheap shovel from Cheap Shovels, Inc. I took down the address and sent off my busted blade, demanding a replacement shovel. Then I shoveled the walk and sat on the steps, waiting for people to come by, thinking about option (*f*) sell house, move to Panama. No one came for hours. I had done this all for naught. Finally the mailman appeared, cutting across the lawn, as usual. I brandished the broken shovel and forced him to use the sidewalk.

He was a little shaken up. Can't wait until the day he delivers my replacement shovel.

Hank the Tree

I AM NOT IN THE HOLIDAY MOOD. YET. IT'S LIKE THIS every year: I spend the first two weeks of December thinking bah and humbug, resisting all attempts to strong-arm me into saying, "ho, ho, ho." Then bells go off, something clicks. I suddenly want to bellyflop into a vat of eggnog, hoist mugs of wassail, charge gifts at ruinous interest rates. Until that day, however, Santa is as welcome as a visit from one's probation officer. *No, I ain't been naughty. Yeah, I been nice. Can I go now?*

This is why I am slightly confused by the presence of a tree in my living room. Every day I have lived in this house, the living room has been free of large coniferous vegetation. Never when I arose in the morning and stumbled downstairs for coffee did it occur to me that there might be a tree waiting for me. But when I saw it the other morning I nearly screamed and ran upstairs to warn my wife: *A tree got in the house last night!* I almost grabbed a tennis racket to beat it out the door.

Part of the problem was that we hadn't yet decorated it. Both of us had too much work to do, and we wanted the first tree-trimming of our married life to be more than dumping a box of ornaments over the tree and sweeping up whatever didn't take. The only thing we had time to do was name it. The tree is now called Hank.

Not all of you are like this, I know. Most people decorate the tree the minute they get it home. (Although everyone names their trees. Right?) But we are alike in one way: we all have an ideal tree in our heads, a template of perfection no real tree can match. A trip to the tree lot is a lesson in impromptu compromising. When Sara and I went to the YMCA lot to buy our tree, we went through all the usual steps. Such as:

1. CHOOSING A BREED. A YMCA volunteer pointed to a Frazier fir and smiled with pride. "That is the Cadillac of firs," he said. "They were specially bred not to shed their needles."

Cadillac, indeed. The Frazier fir cost $60. For that price, it should not only avoid shedding, but walk itself out to the trash on January 2nd. More than the price bothered me; the idea of a eugenically perfect tree was a little disquieting. No Master Race Trees in our house, thank you. It spoils Christmas to wake up and find your Übertannenbaum has annexed the yard and is ordering the elms to move along.

Aside from firs, Christmas trees come in two basic types: spruces and pines. Spruces have stubby, bristly needles; pines have long, thin needles. Your preference for one or the other depends solely on what you grew up with. My family always had a spruce—it said so on the box—and so did Sara's, so neither of us had to betray our childhood. Spruce it would be.

2. CHOOSING A SIZE. Stalking the lot was a shifty-eyed young man, giving each tree no more than a quick glance, pacing the rows, head darting around. I would have thought he had left a tree here for safekeeping, lost it, and was now trying to find it, but his gaze was too impatient. Then he found the Table Trees section and relaxed. He picked one tree after another, scrutinized it, dropped it, hoisted another into the air. Finally he produced a tape measure, pulled out a length of yellow ribbon, and held it up against the trees. "Ahh!" he said to himself. "Perfect."

I had the feeling he was going to use that tree for some unspeakable experiment. He had that look. Like he'd gotten up that morning and said, "Can trees feel pain? And how much?" First stop, hacksaw store. Second stop, tree lot.

But at least he knew exactly what he wanted. Most of us prop the tree on its butt (that is the technical term for the end of the trunk, incidentally) and attempt to imagine it in our homes. You think you have the right size, then you get it home and find you've bought a tree with a pituitary disorder.

Sara found a charming tree in the spruce department; unfortunately, it was about the size of a tree in a model railroad landscape. But next to it was a tree that looked us straight in the eye. Given that both my wife and myself are of bonsai height, this was not a difficult task for the tree. It was the best candidate so far—but one test remained.

3. PROPORTION. We all want our trees to be perfectly conical. Why, I don't know; the first thing one does is stick it in a corner. Half the tree could be missing and no one would know. But *you* would know. So you stand there in the lot, spinning the tree around, checking for flaws. I watched one young couple exalt over the noble size of a Douglas fir, only to let it drop in disgust after examination revealed a gape on one side. I guessed that they were going to put their tree in front of the window and were tremendously socially insecure. They'd look at the gape before they put the flawed side for all the neighbors to see.

Artificial trees were made for these folk.

Sara and I hauled Hank over to the shack; I paid up and the volunteer helped us stuff the tree into the trunk. For a minute I felt bad for the tree. For all the trees. For me, the tree lot was a pleasant place of friendly smells, of ritual and festivity. To the trees it is a slaughterhouse, an abattoir of the forest.

Look at it from the tree's point of view. The poor thing had spent two pleasant years in a nursery, then another three years standing around with its pals, hanging out. One day someone comes and saws it off at the base; for the first time, the tree is parallel to the ground. This cannot be pleasant.

And where does it end up? In a lot with several hundred other trees in similarly dire conditions. *Nothing good is going to come of this,* the tree thinks. *We are all in very big trouble.* After a while, someone takes it away, stuffs it in the trunk like someone who has ratted on the mob, and takes it to a house. What's the first thing the tree sees upon entering the house? Wood. *Dead* wood, everywhere. On the floors, over the doors, made into tables. *I am among savages,* the tree thinks.

The tree assumes it will be soon be sawed, lacquered, and hammered. But no. The people decorate it, light it, feed it water, venerate it. For a while the tree thinks it is being set up for some sort of sacrifice, like the maiden who is made beautiful before she is fed to the giant monkey. But as the days pass and no harm comes to the tree, it begins to believe that it is being worshipped.

That is why the tree always looks so good on Christmas. By then, it thinks that the celebration is for its benefit.

Imagine its shock when it is deposed without ceremony and tossed onto the boulevard. Anger is first—*Oh, I'm not good enough to be used in your floors, is that it? Fine.* This gives way to humiliation, as the tree lies there and looks up at all the trees standing along the street, their roots deep in the ground.

This won't happen with Hank. First of all, Sara went out of her way to make him feel secure—a warm blanket, a ticking clock, the whole works. And since I was initially diffident, he won't get a swelled head when we start to pile on the decorations.

Best of all, he won't go out on the boulevard for the trashman. Hank will not be abandoned. The brochure I got at the tree lot explains that the branches and trunk may be used as mulch or fuel, and that the needles make aromatic sachets. "Your tree," the brochure points out, "is biodegradable."

Really? A biodegradable tree? What *will* they come up with next.

Compost or Die

▬▬▬▬▬▬▬▬▬▬▬▬▬▬▬▬▬▬▬▬

COMPOST OR DIE. NO MORE PUTTING THE GRASS CLIPPINGS out for the trashman, unless you want to spend all night stuffing it into milk cartons. From now on, until the moon is officially opened as a landfill, yard waste has to be composted at home—there's a use for that spare room!—or schlepped to the municipal heap.

Don't know how to get to the municipal heap? Simple. Follow your nose. Drive north until you see people passed out on their lawns, their children sprawled glassy-eyed over the handlebars of their trikes; turn left at the block where the houses have bricked up windows and blistered paint. You'll see a man waving a sharp stick—that's what he uses to wake up the people who have passed out while disposing of yard waste.

I know composting is a good idea. I also believe it is a plot fostered by the hand-held car vacuum cleaner industry. What really burns my grits, though, is the fact that my lawn is only 3.7 percent grass. The rest is weeds. So now I not only have to go out and shave the intruding flora, I have to drive three miles to get rid of it. Next thing you know, the quackgrass will refuse to get into the car unless it can ride shotgun.

If I sound aggravated, I am. Mowing one's lawn is sup-

posed to be a happy chore—you stride across your land
pushing thunder before you, a trail of awed and dominated
grass behind you. The first mow of this season was full of
aggravation, and composting was the least of it.

By last Sunday I knew I should mow. Jeff, my neighbor,
had already mowed and begun the weekly dialogue of where
each of us thinks the property line is. My grass was shin-
high, and there were weeds that looked like they could beat
me at arm-wrestling. Besides, all day long I'd seen men with
gas cans trudging to the corner Gas-o-Mart-o-Rama, looking
like a bucket brigade made up of pyromaniacs. It was time
I mowed.

I went out to the garage and found the mower huddled in
the corner like a hibernating animal. It had somehow built
a thicket of bikes, rakes, brooms, and bags of rock salt
around itself. I disassembled its burrow and hauled it into
the sunlight. The mower caught on the first pull, choked,
convulsed, spat, and died. I tried again, and the motor took.
I, Lawn God, strode manfully into my domain. Destroyer
of Weeds, Defender of Property Values, the Confounder of
Thistles: Lawn God.

Soon all the familiar emotions of lawn mowing returned.
All the hate I feel for weeds, all the glee I feel at seeing
those decapitated dandelion noggins flying out the side of
the mower. Unfortunately, by the time I made a return pass,
the dandelions had completely grown back. During the rainy
weeks they had grown strenuously—if you put your ear to
the ground, you could actually hear them grunting—and they
were not about to be dislodged. I shut off the mower and
fetched some plastic garden edging, the stuff you use to mark
off flower beds. I surrounded the dandelion patch with the
edging, thereby making the dandelions, technically, flowers.
This meant they would all die for no good reason within a
week. I continued to mow.

I next encountered a great amount of dog leavings on the
boulevard. This was a mystery: I had neither seen the dogs
responsible nor heard them. Apparently there was nearby a
huge kennel of mute, stealthy, and ravenous dogs specially

bred for incontinence; their owners fed them heaping platters of chili peppers and jalapeños, and then showed them a map to my house.

My yard, in fact, was littered with all manner of junk. That's the thing about living on a corner lot: you don't just see the parade of life go by, you get to clean up after it. Since, for example, I live close to the aforementioned Gas-o-Mart-o-Rama, I have a carpet of losing lottery tickets on my lawn, a testament to the steep odds. Every time I see the GET YOUR TICKETS HERE sign at the store, I look for the addendum that says AND THROW THEM AWAY BY THE HOUSE A BLOCK UP THE STREET.

A less inventive man would have stooped, picked up the lottery tickets, and separated them from the yard waste. After all, we're all composting this year, partly because we all love the environment, and mostly because the city has announced it will hold public disembowelings of anyone who puts the lawn clippings out with the garbage. Now, it's true that lottery tickets do not qualify as yard waste. On the other hand, if you go over something enough times with the mower, it *becomes* yard waste. I have a busted water heater I plan on composting by just this method. It's cheaper than having it hauled away.

In fact, if you have a mower like mine, you may have no grass to compost. My mower has no bag; it simply spews grass out its left armpit. The shaved grass collects in little rows, and then you mow over those rows. You repeat the process until the entire neighborhood is awash in atomized chlorophyll, and you are coated with grass particles. Passersby see this green creature pushing the mower, and assume it's some weed genetically engineered to mow the lawn.

God forbid I should ever drop dead while I mow; they'd have to bury me in the compost heap. Or face a steep fine.

Groomsmen and
Other Drunks

AS A PROFESSIONAL SHORT PERSON, I AM IN GREAT DEMAND as a groomsman. I lend balance to the event. I'm the squirt on the end who compensates for the best man, who is always about nine feet tall. Why we have to line up according to height, I don't know; the result always looks like a chart on the Ascent of Man, with me playing the role of Neanderthal. Albeit a well-dressed one.

Since it's wedding season, I thought I would pass along my experience for those about to be groomsmen—in particular, what a GM should *not* do. I had a GM gig last week and had a great time. I know I had a great time, because: (*a*) the guy at the tux rental shop said he'd never seen stains like that before; and (*b*) people tell me I gave the arresting officer a really clever alias.

I exaggerate, to be honest. But you know what I mean: slap a tux on your average Joe and it's like handing him a license to corrode his liver. I've seen guys tie one on during the fitting for a tux. One guy came out of the changing room conversing with the reflection in his shoes.

Why this is, I don't know. But this suspension of good sense pervades all the GM's actions. Some groomsmen think their first duty is to fly the groom to Tijuana, hit him on the head, pin a fifty to his shirt and shove him in a bordello. These guys believe that going to a strip joint somehow sanctifies an engagement, as though one must be married in the eyes of God, Man, and Tiffany Del Fumba.

My groomsmen did this to me. They even sprang for something called the Wedding Special, in which the groom sits fish-mouthed while a dozen refugees from a silicon trade show parade around him at a distance mandated by local ordinances. I sat there mortified, saddened not only by the cheap and tawdry nature of the event, but by the knowledge that there was no way I could get out to my car and fetch my camera.

But it's the day of the wedding when the groomsmen are really put to the test. Their first job is to vanish prior to the ceremony and materialize in a bar across town. Scientists have not figured out how this is accomplished, but the moment the photographer signals that he's done with the groomsmen, they evaporate and are reconstituted at Foxy's Tap. This is of great consternation to the bridesmaids, who have been living in the church basement, fully dressed in their gowns, since the bride announced her engagement.

Next, the groomsmen have to find their way back to the church. The canny groomsmen have left a trail of shredded corsage fragments, and everyone follows. Once the GMs are at the church, they have to find the groom and pepper him with questions. Such as: *Nervous? Nervous yet? Nervous at all? Worried about tripping like you did in the rehearsal? Nervous? Last chance to run away, ha ha ha! Nervous?*

Now, the ceremony. The first thing the GM does is walk down the aisle with a friend of the bride. (Usually the bride chooses her bridesmaids; it's not considered correct for the groom to pack the bridesmaid side with women the bride has never met; nor can he refer to them as "spares," or "the bench.") In a touching moment that symbolizes the permanent rite of marriage, the groomsman links arms with a woman he met the previous night at the rehearsal, walks a short way and then splits to be with the guys.

Once the yobs are aligned along the altar, the ceremony

begins. It is now time to be solemn. No making faces at the groom. No waving to people in the pews, mouthing Hi, Mom! or holding up a sign that reads JOHN 3:16.

Not all men deal well with this enforced solemnity, of course. The wedding I recently attended was a fine example. During the opening song, one of the GMs cracked a joke, and all of us were struck with convulsive, silent laughter. From behind, we looked like we were starting to cry, and I'm certain the folks in the pew were touched. I just dread the day the newlyweds see the videotape of the ceremony, and see that all six of us were biting our cheeks and looking cross-eyed.

As irreverent as the GM can be, all pretense and poses are dropped when the couple is finally pronounced man and wife. At that moment, each man feels a sweet sadness, a sense of pride that his buddy has negotiated his way through another of the passages of life, a tang of regret at the realization that we're not kids anymore, we're adults. But the smile on the couple's face wipes the regret from your heart, and the GM stands there, heart full of benevolence. The tux is a uniform, the wedding a campaign, and everyone made it out alive.

Then the GM takes the bridesmaid's hand and walks down the aisle, preparing for his next duty. The banquet is next, and the GM will be expected to tell a story that humiliates the groom in front of two sets of parents.

If everyone is looking down at their plates before you even get to the part about Tijuana, you're doing an excellent job.

I Stand Accused
of Barbicide

I HAVEN'T HAD A HAIRCUT IN EIGHT MONTHS. IT'S LONG enough for a ponytail. Not that I've tried: the minute I gather my hair into a ponytail, my father, who lives 250 miles away, will suddenly sit upright in his lounger and utter a horrible wail. Just as mothers know when their children are in danger, fathers know when their sons are pulling their hair back and fastening them with colorful pieces of elastic.

I'd like to get my hair cut; I really would. Every morning it takes more and more of my wife's goop—that's actually the brand name, Wife Goop—to get the hair to stay down. It would be cheaper to get a paint brush and a gallon of shellac. Several months of this have given my hair the gentle bounce of high-tension wires. If I want a trim, I'll have to go to a metalworking shop and ask to use their bolt cutter.

Barring that, there are three types of places I could go to. And none of them is any fun.

THE BASIC BARBER SHOP. These are the places with names like Harvey's Scissor Shack. There's a painting of a stag on the wall, well-thumbed copies of *True Carburetor Tales,* and two ancient and possibly mummified barbers sitting in the corner, gathering dust. Harvey, who is unnaturally cheerful, is always cutting the hair of a big, beefy guy who runs an insurance agency around the corner. Advantages: you can always get in right away. Disadvantages: you'll get one of the old barbers, who will make you look like you had an accident with the Weed Whacker.

WAREHOUSE O' SHAVING. The volume salons. This is where my wife goes; it only costs a few bucks, and she always looks wonderful. Then again, my wife could go to Crazed-Blind-Man-Waving-A-Machete Salon and she'd look great. Years of paying too much for a stylist who is rarely available has made me suspicious. The sign WALK-INS WELCOME says to me INCAPABLE OF GENERATING REPEAT BUSINESS. Advantages: low cost, chance of getting a genius just out of school. Disadvantages: pressure to work quickly leads to many cases of stylists inadvertently pithing customer when doing the neck.

NEEDLESSLY HIP STYLISTS. The stark decor, the pounding music, the skittish stylists who believe that just as Michelangelo worked in stone, they work in *hair*. Advantages: stylists swap lurid gossip between themselves; constant parade of good-looking people. Disadvantages: staff makes fun of you after you leave; stylist frequently begs to sign and date the haircut if he or she believes it is a really good one.

That's the kind of place I've been going to, but not anymore. The last genius I hired to cut my hair seemed to believe I was paying him $25 to tell me about his vacation. Each story required that he make a series of elaborate gestures. I would look up into the mirror and see this guy waving a scissors and a comb as if he were summoning up the voodoo gods in charge of barbering. And he always insisted on washing my hair. Never mind that I had washed it no more than a half hour before; to his eyes, I had been held by the ankles and dipped in roofing tar just prior to walking into his shop.

It was not always so. For eight years I had a stylist with the character of a bartender: if you wanted to talk, she listened; if you asked for an honest opinion, she lied. "Am I getting balder?" I'd ask, knowing full well my hairline was a few years away from being called my neck. She would say I looked no balder than the last visit; in fact—and here she would pull out the script I had handed her upon my first visit to the salon—"you look more hairy and virile than ever, you *man* you."

One day she moved to a distant suburb. She still expected me to come to her to get my hair cut. *Sure. I think Braniff has a shuttle I can catch.* I never went, of course. Eventually she sent me a nasty letter, with a thick sheaf of photographs: eight years of overhead shots of my head, arranged chronologically, with little black lines marking off the yearly hair loss.

Since then, I've never stayed too long with one stylist. They either vanish and send preprinted postcards saying, "Hi! I have, for no apparent reason, changed salons!" or make me want to commit Barbicide. Either way, I eventually end up stranded.

Perhaps I should forget it and grow my hair out long. Women with long hair, I've noted, are apparently required to pick it up and throw it over their shoulders every ninety seconds. Looks like fun, and I could use the exercise.

April the 15th

TAXES USED TO BE EASY. I MADE NO MONEY, AND THE government took half of it. I never made enough to fill out the 1040EZ; I used the 1040LA, which is for liberal arts graduates. It's the only tax form that allows you to write off phone calls to your parents in which you ask for money.

But I am an adult now, with adult-sized responsibilities. I tried to do my taxes by myself this year, and I ended up owing a figure that looked like Scrooge McDuck's net worth. I managed to owe more than I made. That couldn't be right. I got out the phone book, looked up the Taxpayer Assistance division of the IRS. Their motto: "Persuading Taxpayers to Round Numbers Up for Over Sixty Years—Make That Seventy."

"IRS Taxpayer Assistance, Isabel speaking, how can I influence your return?"

"I seem to owe more than I made last year," I asked. "Is that possible?"

"Yes," said Isabel. "Most people owe more than they made, and lie about it. That's why we're building more prisons."

"Thank you."

"Not at all."

Well, I'd have none of that. Just as there are no atheists in a foxhole, there are no altruists on April 15th. I needed the help of a professional, someone who could wrestle my return to the ground and make it yield. All the reputable ones were booked solid, however; the only place that could squeeze me in was Bob's Twenty-Minute EZ Lube and Tax Preparation. I asked the receptionist if, like the other tax-preparation firms, they paid any penalties incurred by filing an inaccurate return. She said no, but if I had to go to jail they would help me pack. Good enough. I made an appointment.

"Lube job or taxes?" asked the receptionist when I arrived. I told her I didn't really see the difference between the two, but I was here to speak to Bob about my return. Bob was tied up, the receptionist said, and was not expected in the office for five to seven years; Jacko would help me. I was led me to a small room where a wiry man stood at the window, peering through the blinds, smoking a cigarette. This, presumably, was Jacko. When the receptionist had left, he closed the blinds, removed his sunglasses, and sized me up.

"Lemme see your receipts," he said.

I had feared this. Unlike my wife, who has receipts from gumball machines she patronized ten years ago and, if pressed, could probably document all of her past lives to the satisfaction of an IRS agent, I am incapable of saving important pieces of paper. If they tattooed the receipt on my arm, I'd stick it in a threshing machine on the way home. In my single days, I had kept records by taping the pieces of paper to a milk carton and putting it in the fridge, where I knew it would be at the year's end. But somehow I had no records for 1989. Jacko shrugged, said it was no problem, and examined the first draft of my 1040.

"What is this?" he finally said. "Uncle Sam's been choppin' off half yer kielbasa every other week for the last year, and you want to give him more? You nuts or what? Play ball, kid, and I'll get you a refund so big you'll be lightin' yer smokes with C-notes."

"Well, if it's legal, sure."

"I'm doin' you a favor here," Jacko said, his voice cold. "You got a problem with that?" I said we had none. We proceeded.

"First of all, we get you the Injured Spouse deduction." He made a check mark on my form. I told Jacko that neither my wife nor myself was infirm, but he waved off the objection. "If you get audited, we send somebody around to break your leg. Part of the service."

I told him I appreciated their attention.

"If you feel that way, we can check off the deduction for bein' blind. Same guarantee." I said no. "Okay. Now. Charitable contributions. Let's put ten grand. You don't need receipts here—we can say you gave it to beggars. Lemme see . . . gambling losses. Let's deduct fifteen grand."

"Jacko," I said, "according to what you're putting down, I spent most of 1989 stuffing fifties into the shirt pockets of panhandlers and playing three-card monte."

"You're right. You're disturbed. *Thirty* grand for shrink's bills. And as long as we're on medical expenses, what did you spend for food last year?" I must have looked puzzled. "We can deduct food! You don't eat it, you get sick!"

I decided Jacko was not the man I wanted to prepare my return. Anything he signed would probably make the IRS mobilize their 87TH Airborne Auditing Squad. Twenty men in dark suits would parachute onto my lawn the day they got this return. I excused myself and left the office.

I filled out my taxes on my own, and sent them in. If I get audited, fine; I'll turn state's evidence on Jacko and bargain my way out of it. Would I fear reprisals? Not at all. There's always the Witness Relocation Program. And moving expenses are deductible.

2

THE PUBLIC WORLD

I always wanted to be a columnist. When I was growing up, delivering the *Fargo Forum,* I admired most the people who had their pictures in the paper for reasons other than being arrested. These people got to cork off about whatever they wanted, several times a week. One man, Wayne Lubenow, was my hero: people got mad about what he said, smiled over his work, used his name as casually as one would use the name of one's spouse, or the president.

Trouble is, it takes a lot of work to be anointed a columnist. The normal route is to spend half a decade slogging in the trenches of small-town papers, reporting about sewer-board meetings and cat rescues, after which a major newspaper recognizes your ability and calls you into the big leagues. This moment usually coincides with the total loss of one's ability to be the free-swinging, Lubenowesque columnist one wanted to be, having had all originality ground out of your spirit by writing about sewer-board meetings.

Somehow, I've managed to be a columnist four times in my career—the first time at a college paper that handed that honor out so frequently as to make it as exclusive as membership in the Rosicrucians, the second at an alternative weekly that had pages to fill. My third shot came at the *St. Paul Pioneer Press.*

When I joined the paper, it was already bristling with fine columnists. During my job interview I told the editor that I wanted to be a columnist, and she told me that she had more than enough white male columnists, thank you. Whatever fizzy liquids I wanted to uncork would have to be vented through the feature section.

So I did. Most of the pieces that follow masqueraded as feature articles, when, of course, they were hollering out COLUMN at the top of their lungs. That these things were published as feature pieces is a testament to the editorial leadership of the paper, which did not have an aneurysm whenever the first person was used by a lowly writer. Some of these pieces ran as columns—toward the end of my tenure, I was granted the all-important Picture and Big Byline, and in my mind I took the opportunity to seize up and stammer, flummoxed by the spotlight.

See if you can guess which of these fall into that category.

True Cultural Literacy

━━

ACCORDING TO ALL THE RECENT SURVEYS, EVERY AMERI-
can below the age of eighteen is, and I quote the experts,
"stupid as a shingle." Perhaps that overstates the case a bit,
but you've read the news stories—high-schoolers who
couldn't place World War One in the proper century unless
you spotted them the 1 and the 9, kids who, when asked to
name the continents, stick out their tongue and look puzzled
after putting down "Atlantis" and "North and South Moon."

The reports indicate that this will have far-reaching consequences for Western Civilization, and they're right; those
who don't know the horrors and mistakes of the past are
doomed to repeat it. Proof can be found in the fact that ABC
recently completed casting for "The New Charlie's Angels."
Senselessness like this can be avoided, but it will take a return
to basics.

There's been a good side to the cretins-with-mohawks
story, though: everyone whose formal schooling was completed long ago can lobby hard for tougher schools, knowing
full well they won't have to go through it again. Those calling
for a War on Idiocy, in other words, are past the draft age.
But before we get too smug, we should examine ourselves.
Are we as smart as we would like to be? Probably not. Have

we forgotten much of what we learned? Of course. The day I was graduated from high school, a little spigot opened in my brain and everything I learned about math and chemistry gurgled out, never to return.

Anyone curious to learn just what they have forgotten, and just what the next generation should know, must immediately read *Test Your Cultural Literacy,* by Diane and Kathy Zahler. The Zahlers have put together a compendium of things every well-educated person should know. God bless the Zahlers, this is a multiple-choice quiz.

Here's an example, taken from the Art and Architecture portion.

Question 37: What is this statue? (*a*) *The Sleeping Muse;* (*b*) *Adam;* (*c*) *The Recumbent Figure;* (*d*) *The Thinker.*

(Hint: there is a picture of a man *thinking.*)

That's right! It's *d!*

I know what you're thinking: the quiz is far too hard. There's no way we can expect people to know this stuff. In the interests of a more egalitarian approach to cultural literacy, I have devised the test below, which simultaneously expands and contracts the definition of culture. By which I mean, of course, less history and more TV.

1. Which was the cutest of the sisters on "The Brady Bunch"?
A) Jan
B) Cindy
C) Marsha

2. Which of the following was never referred to as "the fifth Beatle"?
A) Billy Preston
B) George Martin
C) Cardinal Richelieu

3. Which of the following is a continent? Think carefully.
A) Al Jolson singing "Mammy"
B) North America, which certainly looks like a continent
C) A bag containing sticks and old phone books

4. Literature: What is the correct name of entrepreneur Harvey MacKay's first book?
- A) *Swim with the Sharks Without Being Eaten Alive*
- B) *Swim After Eating Without Getting Cramps*
- C) *Tag Along with the Sharks Until They Give You a Blurb*

5. Here is a cubist picture of a nude descending a staircase, or so the artist says. I mean, modern art, who can tell. What is the title of this piece?
- A) *Big Pointless Blobs of Paint* (Robert Motherwell)
- B) *I'm Incredibly Hammered* (Jackson Pollock)
- C) *Nude Descending a Staircase* (Marcel Duchamp)

6. When Louis XIV said, *"L'état c'est moi,"* he was
- A) speaking in French
- B) played by Laurence Olivier in a BBC series
- C) absolutely serious

7. In the classic Doors song "Riders on the Storm," what does the singer *not* feel like?
- A) like an actor out on loan
- B) like facing up to his self-destructive behavior which would, ultimately, lead to his early death
- C) like a dog without a bone

8. Who framed Roger Rabbit?
- A) Foghorn Leghorn
- B) Al Sharpton
- C) Foghorn Sharpton

9. Donald Trump is
- A) famous for introducing fresco painting technique to Northern Europe
- B) famous for buying, and then failing to pay for, all the fresco paintings of Northern Europe
- C) often cited as an argument against the theory of evolution

10. Liposuction is
- A) teenage slang for kissing

55

B) a word certain to be mentioned in the first three sentences
of Cher's obituary
C) Latin for "too lazy to diet"

11. The Greenhouse Effect is caused by
A) too many heat-trapping substances in the atmosphere
B) too many tenure-seeking scientists in the universities
C) Richard Nixon's reappearance on the political scene

12. Radon is
A) just what we here in the media needed to sell some papers
B) the creature that was soundly defeated by Godzilla
C) a colorless, odorless substance you cannot see or taste

13. A presidential candidate is
A) a colorless, odorless substance you cannot see or taste
B) a creature who, confronted by Godzilla, would consult with
his Large Mutated Lizard PAC before advocating action
C) somehow, by sheer coincidence, always a white male

14. A quark is
A) Appalachian pronunciation for an idiosyncrasy, as in
"makin' hogs squeal out lawd for fun is just one'a his
personal quarks"
B) a theoretical particle whose existence can only be hypoth-
esized, not proven (*see also* Cathy Lee Crosby, talent of)
C) An important part of a balanced breakfast

15. Dick Clark looks perpetually young because
A) he sold his soul to the devil
B) the devil does all his makeup and handles the lighting
C) he is the devil

16. The Van Allen belt is
A) a band of radiation surrounding the earth
B) rapidly being replaced by the more stylish Van Allen
suspenders
C) what Van Allen has at the bar after a hard day

17. Which of the following was not a catchphrase taken from
television?

A) "Na-nu na-nu"
B) "Dy-no-*mite!*"
C) "Unstrap that careless butter salesman, Agnes"

18. How many amendments are there to the Constitution?
A) how many do you want?
B) fourscore and seven
C) 33⅓

19. In the event the president is incapacitated, who takes over
    the presidency?
A) Jay Leno
B) the Lucky Charms leprechaun
C) Harold Stassen (it's only fair)

20. What is the point of cultural literacy?
A) not being shown up at parties by geeks who actually studied
    in school
B) smug pride in your own collection of arcane facts
C) having a basis of shared knowledge and ideas that facilitate
    the advancement of intellectual discussion

The answer to all of the above, with the exception of the
last question, is *D*. You will notice that none of the questions
has *D* for an answer. If you answered any of the questions,
you are culturally illiterate.

Please pick up your high school diploma at the door.

Highlights of
Adult Education

Your local Adult Education Division ("Teaching the Bored How to Focus a Camera for Over Fifty Years") is pleased to announce the following lineup of fall classes. Please register early, as enrollment is limited. Theoretically, at least. I mean, Einstein says that space eventually curves back on itself, although no one has ever seen this happen. Likewise, no one has ever been turned away from a class. But it *could* happen. Really.

Oh, all right, just show up the first day with your checkbook.

Here are some of your choices:

COOKING 4367: THE LOST SECRETS OF THE FRANCHISE CHAINS. The class will learn recipes for all those items in fast-food restaurants that are available for "a limited time only." Chef Bob Anderson has a been a fry cook at all the major chains in a variety of cities and has collected the recipes for over ten years' worth of promotional food items. The class concludes with a field trip to a local fast-food restaurant where Chef Bob recently worked; the entire class will request an item no longer on the menu and Chef Bob will shout at the manager that he bets he wished he hadn't fired Bob, nosiree, old Bob would come in pretty handy now, wouldn't he? Tuesdays, 3:00 P.M. to 11:30 P.M. Cost: $50 (includes beverage).

LANGUAGES 2032: FRENCH THE EASY WAY. Students will learn how to speak English with a French accent. Instructor Robert (pronounced Rho-*ber*) Anderson will prepare the student for a trip to France, where, as he puts it, "no one listens to you anyway, so why bother." Wednesdays, 3:00–3:05 P.M. Cost: a fistful of that funny-looking stuff the Frogs call money.

LANGUAGES 2033: ADVANCED FRENCH THE EASY WAY. Same as 2032, except you learn how to say everything louder.

PHILOSOPHY 0000: WESTERN THOUGHT AS EXPRESSED THROUGH DURUM WHEAT PRODUCTS. Since the introduction of letter-shaped macaroni in the early '50s, many people have taken comfort in the sight of a homespun maxim spelled out in pasta and glued to a board. Instructor Mary Johnson-Anderson, who has been gluing macaroni letters to pieces of scrap wood for over twenty years and forcing the results on friends, was the author of "A House Is A House, But A Home Is A Home," which won a first place in the Best Tautology, Crafts Division, of the 1974 Montana State Fair. She will teach the class such skills as how to make an *F* out of an *E*. Students must supply their own aphorism. Thursdays, 7:00 P.M. until your eyes water and your head throbs. Cost: Oh, she just does it for the fun of making something, she couldn't take money—although a coffee cake would be nice.

INVESTMENT 9049: HOW TO LOSE AT THE LOTTERY. Gambling whiz R. "Lucky" Anderson addresses the needs of the gambler who's tired of scratching off his lottery ticket only to find that he's won money *again*. "Despite what the experts tell you," says Lucky, "it's very *easy* to lose money on the lottery. And I'm here to show you how." Techniques include: Turning in that winning ticket for more tickets, right away; Carry only twenties, buy a lot of candy bars, and take your change in tickets. Lucky will also address the question "Scratching them off as soon as you buy them or doing it outside the convenience store: Which is more pathetic?" Fridays, either 3:00, 4:00, or 5:00—take your chances! Cost: your weight in pull tabs.

PHILOSOPHY 4333: CONDUNDRUMS—CONDRUN-DUMS—AW, HELL, JUST CALL 'EM MYSTERIES. Let's get metaphysical! A panel of experts, including acclaimed lecturer Fred from the Ford plant, and noted drinker Bobby Anderson, ponder life's unexplainable elements. A different lecture each week. Topics include:

- "Why are things sometimes closer than they appear in the mirror? There's a problem at the mirror factory, maybe?"
- "Wieners come in packs of ten, buns in packs of eight, beer in packs of six, presliced bologna comes in packs of sixteen slices, condoms come in packs of 3. Jesus H., why can't they get it straight? Man needs a calculator just to have a weekend."
- "Why aren't there any prizes in bran cereals? Or flavored marshmallow bits? As long as we're on the subject, if Tony the Tiger met the leprechaun from Lucky Charms, would he eat him, or is there like a cartoon cereal spokesman's union?"
- "Why can't it be both 'Tastes Great' *and* 'Less Filling'?"
- "How do they arrange it so the last day of the fair is always Labor Day?"
- "Remember those sticky wallwalker things—throw 'em at the wall and they walk down? Well, they said they sold about thirty million of 'em. So: *Where did they all go?*"

Saturdays, 9:00 P.M. to closing. Cost: a round. Hey, it may not be education, but it's certainly adult.

Rap Music,
Explained

━━━━━━━━━━━━━━━━━━━━━━━━━━

I'M GETTING USED TO RAP MUSIC IN COMMERCIALS BUT WAS
nonetheless surprised to see it used in a spot for a cemetery.
"When the old Grim Reaper come to get what you got," an
angry, insistent voice chanted, "they gotta drop your booty
in a burial plot. Eternity Garden: for when you bust this vale
of tears."

Rap is the dominant form of popular music nowadays,
and it's everywhere. I wanted to hate it—unlike the music
of my youth, which was performed by pimply, pop-eyed an-
archists or clever young drunks in thrift-store suits—rap has
virtually no melody, no instrumental breaks or solos. It's the
pop song after a trip to the chop shop: stripped down and
easy to sell. Since it's the music of people younger than
myself, I feel obligated, as a balding, wrinkle-obsessed,
mortgage-burdened adult, to condemn it.

But I like it. Sure, most rap is performed by ranting
boneheads, but the bonehead quotient is high in every musical genre. I do know that it sets your feet on fire, and that's
all that matters. Nevertheless, I know that there are thousands of you who recoil in horror when presented with rap.
It's so . . . aggressive. So . . . strange. So . . . go on, say it:
so *black*.

That it is. But black music for years has been American popular music, provided that whites were performing it. (If Elvis Presley had been black, there would be no rumors about his still being alive, because we'd have the photographs of his lynching.) Rap is simply what's been at the roots of popular music for the better part of this century, and it's only fair that rap gets its chance to be the soundtrack of America. By 1997, of course, it will be discarded by a new batch of oversexed limber-limbed youths, and something else will take its place. Probably ragtime.

Until then, there are millions of you who are still confused by rap, what it means and what they are talking about. Allow me to answer some common questions and fears.

WHAT ARE MOST RAP SONGS ABOUT? Most songs deal with the passionate and loving relationship between the rapper and himself. The point of the rap song is to tell you how good the rapper is, and to exalt the moment when he actually grabs the mike. Translated into, say, a country western song, the lyrics would be:

> *I'm singin' a song to this microphone, darlin'.*
> *I'm singin' a song, and I'm good, yessirree.*
> *Well I'm singin' right now, it's a song that I'm singin',*
> *And no one is better than me, yee hah.*

There is a strange, almost metaphysical dimension to this lyrical content. Most rappers, in describing their prowess at rapping, refer to performances in which they were superior —but since *all* their performances consist of describing this example of perfection, they are probably referring to some theoretical or ideal performance.

WHAT ARE "SUCKAS"? Ah. You have been paying attention. Most rappers refer to "suckas," as in "suckas scatter when I grab the mike." The "suckas" (singular: sucka) is a variety of inferior rapper who, when presented with a superior talent, inevitably slinks away in defeat. Studies have shown, however, that the original Sucka is probably mythical. Since every rapper describes his power over suckas, and since no rapper ever admits to having been, at one time, a sucka, there cannot possibly be enough suckas to go around.

Curiously enough, there was word a few years ago of an Anti-Sucka Defamation League being formed, but someone grabbed a mike, and they scattered.

CAN RAP BE USED FOR EDUCATIONAL PURPOSES? Not really. You hear a great deal about teaching kids history or math with rap, but it's difficult to express complex ideas in rhyming couplets. "The Renaissance made all the feudal suckas scatter / 'cause the new groove was: It's Man that matters" doesn't do justice to the shift in postmedieval thought. Nor can difficult disciplines, such as medicine, be explained through rap. "I rock the mike," for example, tells an audience that you are a good rapper. "I rock the bone saw" does not tell the patient that you are a good surgeon.

WHY DO I HEAR SNIPPETS OF OLD SONGS IN RAP TUNES? That's called sampling, or using a computer to xerox a piece of music and paste it into your tune. MC Hammer's "U Can't Touch This" swipes the hard groove from Rick James's "Superfreak" of the previous decade. Next year, MC Needle-Nose Pliers will sample from MC Hammer; the year after that, MC Craftsman 32-Piece Socket Wrench will sample from his predecessor. This is how music is kept fresh.

I hope this makes things clear. If not, stand up quickly. Did you hear a loud, sharp crack? Was it your knees? If so, you are excused from appreciating rap. If not, you are hereby commanded to look past the nonsense and start dancing. If you can't bring yourself to do that, go face a mirror and shout, "Turn that racket down!" Feel old? You are. In a few years, that Sex Pistols album will be background music for a Geritol ad. ("Oi Am An Anarchist! And Oi've Got Lumbago!") But this means that *twenty* years from now, rap will serve the same function. There will be a radio station for old people that plays nothing but rap. And when they shout, "Bust a hip joint, y'all," they really mean it. This too will pass.

Take heart: something truly worse will take its place.

How to Be Driven Mad
by Literature

The main consolation of having a novel published is the knowledge that it will probably sink out of sight.

That wasn't exactly how my editor put it, but that was the essence of the issue. She told me that first novels rarely do well, and for every *Bright Lights, Big City* there are dozens of deserving books that wither on the shelves. I suggested retitling my book *Brighter Lights, Even Bigger City* but she shook her head. My book would have to stand on its merits, face alone the caprices of the marketplace. Not that it was doomed to fail, certainly not, anything can happen, but . . . here, order another drink. The company's paying. Of course, it's coming out of the publicity budget, so if you want any ads, order the bar pour.

So the book was doomed. I did the only thing that felt right. I wept with relief and thanked God.

In order that you may better understand my misery, some insights on how a novel is published.

1. ACTUALLY WRITING THE BOOK. You do not have to write a book to sell one. This is one of the nicest facts about the book industry. You give them an outline, a few sample chapters, and they start throwing, oh, tens of dollars at you. They offer you a contract, which at that point is thicker than your book; the contract gives them complete control of your life for the right to print enough copies of your book to give to overworked, cynical book reviewers. Your agent goes *mano a mano* with the publisher, engaging in bitter fights over things like first serial rights on novelty bathroom tissue.

Eventually, you end up with a contract that gives the publisher the right to publish the book, the author the right to stop it from being made into a movie starring Dudley Moore, and New Zealanders the right to show up on your doorstep and punch you because they just don't like your posture in the jacket photo.

After the contract is completed, you have to write the book. First, you spend all the money they have given you so far. Then, you sharpen your pencils—even if you work with a word processor, you need something with a point to jab into your forearm and keep you awake while you desperately attempt to meet the deadline. If you miss the deadline, two burly men in good suits show up and intimidate you. "Nice subplot you got there," the smaller one will say, while the burly one toys with the delete key. "Shame if anything *happened* to it."

You finish the book, make thirty-eight copies, and mail it off. Postal and copying costs so far: one-fifth of your advance.

2. THE BOOK IS HACKED TO SHREDS. My book came back whimpering and bleeding. If it had been a horse, I would have shot it. I noted that the postage was forty-eight cents more than it had cost to mail it—the added weight of the corrections, I soon learned. There were two pages of instructions that read like the adjustments on a fifty-four-band graphic equalizer. Entire chapters were cut out; minor characters were poked into limbo. There was a suggestion that two characters who did not like each other should sleep together, in order to add Tabasco to the latter half of the book. I had to get them drunk to do it.

I followed the editorial suggestions, of course. When an editor writes, "I think the flowers on the table in chapter twelve should be roses instead of mums," the author reads,

"I think the flowers on the table in chapter twelve should be roses instead of mums, OR WE WON'T PUBLISH YOUR STUPID PATHETIC NOVEL!" The entire process starts to feel like torture, as though you have found yourself remanded to the Department for Pulling Out Fingernails for the Hell of It. You endure, do what they say, and hope there might be a Nuremberg trial for editors. Then again, you too could be hanged for following orders.

I boxed up the book, made thirty-eight copies, mailed it off. The postage was less, as I had shaved 136 pages off the manuscript. But this was matched by the cost of two bottles of Scotch, absorbed while I endured the editor's notes in the margins.

3. THE COPY EDITOR'S VERSION. After a few months, a third version of the book arrived, this one bearing the commentary of the copy editor. These people have long been the bane of my life; they are impossibly literal. Had God been a copy editor, the Ten Commandments would have all been laws of grammar, and people would today be kneeling in confessionals to admit to wantonly splitting an infinitive.

But they are invaluable, these people; they force writers to face the problems with the world the writers have created, and hence writers resent them immensely.

The copy editor assigned to my book, however, was the apotheosis of copy editors, a genetic experiment in producing a master race of anal-retentive readers. Every page had a little Post-it note with five or six questions—issues of punctuation, grammar, or, my favorite, a question mark next to what I thought was a particularly clever joke.

I became obsessed with this man, with his capacity for detail. First of all, he was clearly a paid agent of the American Comma Board; he insisted on putting commas everywhere, particularly in those sentences, like this one, that rival freight trains for length. He also addressed matters of internal consistency: I had said that the small town of Prosper was south of Valhalla, yet when my main character is driving north, he sees a road sign that reads PROSPER 8, VAHALLA 4. *How can this be?* said the note. I could have corrected this by transposing the numbers, but I was not in a giving mood; I drew up a map whereby I proved that by taking certain roads that did not exist the distance I cited was correct between two towns that were entirely fictional. I slept well that night.

I knelt to his authority on most matters, printed off another version of the book, made thirty-eight copies and mailed it off. Cost so far: another fifth of the advance, plus money spent to hire a detective to tail around the editor and find out what he does wrong so I could send him a few notes.

4. GALLEYS. After a while, the publisher throws caution to the wind and actually sets the book in type. It is then sent to you to proofread, since apparently Mr. Hot Shot Copy Editor can't be troubled with such menial work.

For the first time it looks like a real book. This is when it hits you that you are having a book published, and while it is exciting at first, nausea sets in the minute you start to proofread. You have now read this book more times than anyone ought to and you know every joke, every surprise. You begin to wonder if the book should be printed at all. When you finished it, it was a noble thing of erect posture and beauteous features; now it is a twisted Quasimodo that will shamble down the streets crying out your name and cursing you for sending it naked and defenseless into the world.

You find just enough typos in the book to convince you that you've missed most of them, and then you mail it back. Total cost by now: all of your advance.

5. THE BOOK IS PUBLISHED, OR, WORSE, RE-VIEWED. Several things might happen. It might be given to a reviewer who hates it because it is not set in a trailer park chock full of white trash who eat Fritos and eventually rob gas stations, and thus is not really representative of America. Or, it is not set in New York and populated with anxiety-ridden, coke-addled young book reviewers, and thus is not really representative of America. In either case, you are up against people who are working on novels of their own, and are deeply resentful of you for having published one.

I was lucky. My book sank so fast that, fifty years from

now, I fully expect *National Geographic* to send a bathysphere down to photograph it. I am told that this is typical with first novels, that next time I'll get more publicity, and that will expose more people to my work.

I can only hope this is an idle threat.

Officer, There's a Woman in the Bathroom

■■■■■■■■■■■■■■■■■■■■■■■■■■■■■■■

BACK IN THE DAYS WHEN THE EQUAL RIGHTS AMENDMENT was being debated, certain cretinous elements were convinced that the guiding tenet of the law was to create unisex bathrooms. Never mind that most women regard the very concept of a restroom devoted entirely to men as a hygienic horror they would not enter without tongs, fifty gallons of bleach, and a lead-lined suit; some men envisioned hordes of braless, hairy-legged women beating down the doors of men's rooms all across the country, just to make a point. If not see one. The bad old days of desegregation, all over again: National Guardsmen escorting women into men's bathrooms, Lester Maddox standing in front of a bathroom door, waving a plunger.

The ERA failed, but unisex bathrooms are a *de facto* reality. Consider the case of Denise Wells, arrested in Houston in 1990 for using the men's room. She was at a country-western concert, and, perhaps because most of the songs in C&W deal with beer, tears, the Rio Grande, and various other flowing fluids, she felt the sudden need to visit the facilities. Unfortunately, the line for the women's room consisted of nearly sixty grim-faced sisters, all knock-kneed with the rigors of self-control. This wouldn't do; her body had sensed porcelain in the vicinity, and was about to state its case. So she ducked into the men's room.

No, there wasn't a policeman in the bathroom; there never is a policeman in the bathroom. They hate for others to see *them* up against a wall, legs apart. But on this night, one of Houston's Finest saw her leaving the Men's Room. He stopped her, gave her a $200 ticket for being in the wrong privy, and kicked her out of the concert hall.

Before you wonder what the world, and specifically Houston, is coming to, you should know that this already happens everywhere. I can't go to the restroom in a nightclub nowadays without finding a half dozen taffeta confections standing in the corner looking snarky, full of naughty hauteur. In New York, which seceded from civilization several years ago, the bathrooms of the clubs are the only place where you can talk without sprouting nodes on your vocal cords, and hence people congregate there: even people who have nothing to say need a place to say it. But in all my days of multigender bathroom visits, I've never seen the cops saunter in, gats drawn, and haul out those whose sex wasn't posted on the door.

Why women are forced into men's bathrooms is no mystery. Architects have long forgotten to take into consideration the basic facts. The average man spends 23.6 seconds in the lavatory—17.3 seconds to accomplish the objective, 3.2 to pretend to wash his hands, and 3.1 attempting to think of a new way to deface the instructions on the hand dryer. Men are generally brisk about the matter; in fact, most start to undo their fly when they leave the table.

Women, on the other hand, take an average of 3.5 hours per visit. Apparently they cannot undo their foundation garments without entering a fifty-digit security code. Add to this the inability of some woman not to look around and start to wonder how *she* would have done the room. This slows things up and leads to long lines.

The fault, of course, lies with the architects. And you get one guess as to the sex of the architects. I suppose we should compliment them for putting in men's rooms at all, when most men would be content with a wall and some shrubs.

I'll be happy when women have enough bathrooms. It's hard on them to stand there staring at the grout on the tiled floor, ears burning so hot you can smell melted hair, happy as animal-rights activists on a tour of a slaughterhouse. It's hard on the shy men who walk in, see women, slink back to their chair and die of uremic poisoning an hour later. It's murder on the guys who are just looking for a place to make loud noises and tell lies.

But this has to work both ways, right? The last time I was at a nightclub, I found the men's room clogged with burly urinators, and the women's room almost empty. I burst into the women's room and proclaimed my delight at the complete and utter devastation of the last pointless barrier between the sexes.

When the police arrived and took me away, the arresting officer was a woman. Strangely enough, she had no sympathy for my position whatsoever. She booked me on a 703. Failure to leave the seat down.

Yes, men: turns out it *is* a crime.

A Survey of
Hangovers

―――――――――――――

THE FOLLOWING IS NOT INTENDED TO BE AN ENDORSEMENT
of drinking. I suppose it *could* be—if you think a description
of a car wreck is meant to be an encouragement to drive fast.
But just as everyone has had a fender bender once or twice,
so have many people woken up after a night of revelry and
felt like a crash dummy at quitting time. It does not mean
one has spent the previous evening hanging from a chandelier
or has passed out face-first in a trough of grain spirits. It
means only that whatever limit you have for absorbing alcohol without deleterious effects, you went over. You may
have gone over by an inch, or you may have done an Olym-
pic-qualifying broad jump. In any case, you are hung over.

The American Society for Hangover Statistics, which I just
invented, says that the holidays are the peak times for hangovers. Indeed, so prevalent is the holiday skullbanger that
the Pentagon fears that all the Soviets need do on the morning of January 1st is surround the country and bang cymbals,
and we would capitulate. The Society notes that changing
attitudes toward alcohol have brought hangover rates down,
but they stress that as a fictitious organization, they cannot
document their data.

It is your author's contention that things have not changed

all that much. There is a segment of the population that never gets a hangover—either because they regard anything on the high side of rum cake to be an object of loathsome moral degeneracy, or because they do not care for the taste or the effect. There is another group of people who drink in moderation but have, once or twice, woken up feeling like they had spent the night riding a lumber wagon loaded with bowling balls. Another portion is so accustomed to a hangover they set a place for it at the breakfast table. They are not reading this piece. The way the type moves up and down hurts their eyes.

Now that we have set the ground rules for discussing this subject, let us examine the common hangover—its manifestations, its reasons for being, and ways to banish it.

The hangover's forms are as many as the evil brews that launch it. Consider the following types of hangovers:

THE QUASIMODO. This is where you wake up with your head feeling as though a giant clapper hangs inside your skull, smashing with metronomical precision into the tender interior of your head. Sufferer walks around hunchbacked, arms swinging, face contorted in pain. Cause: wine, particularly wine sold in boxes or with twist-off caps.

THE EVIL DWARVES. A variation on the Quasi, this version recalls the sensation of having evil sprites set up drilling rigs on your temples. Sound does not cause discomfort, but bright light feels like an ice pick. Sufferer will often insist the blinds not only be drawn but replaced with sheets of lead. Cause: champagne. Next time when you uncork a bottle, just point the bottle at your temple. Death comes quicker that way.

THE LEAPING GORGE. Here the sufferer feels precariously balanced between feeling fine and being instantly and flamboyantly ill. The stomach is like a jack-in-the-box, waiting for the final crank of the handle. Even the conception of sustenance can discomfit, but it depends on the food. A soda cracker, for example, placed fifteen yards away and downwind from the sufferer will probably have no effect, but merely thinking the word "beets" near the afflicted will have

73

untoward consequences. Cause: that from which Milwaukee derives its fame.

THE DO-NOT-ADJUST-YOUR-SET; ALSO CALLED THE TUNING FORK. A disconcerting affliction, as the sufferer is convinced the entire world is vibrating, including him or herself. Vertigo is likely; entering an escalator in this state and looking at the moving steps can induce psychosis. Cause: your obstinate refusal fourteen hours before to say, "No, I think a cup of coffee would be a sensible choice," instead of saying, "Thirteen-year-old peat-cured single-malt Scotch? Never had one! Sure, let me finish this yeasty, dark Belgian beer and then I'll have a double!"

THE I-AM-SCUM. There are, according to the dictionary, psychological reasons for being overhung, but you have to be rather far gone, the type who spends all day sucking anything with a tax stamp, for these to surface. "In alcoholics with a history of repeated destructive and asocial drinking behavior . . . anxiety, guilt, and remorse may play an important role." If you wake up in a strange motel room with the TV wrecked and smoking, a strange tattoo on your arm, a clanging head that recalls the end of "Dragnet," where a sweaty hand smites the letters MARK VII into a plate of steel, and a Visa receipt for a group of hookers listed as "The Magnificent Seven," your hangover could be your conscience whacking you with a two-by-four. Cure: aspirin, then pithing.

How to avoid these hangovers? Simple. The dictionary is helpful: "The only way to avoid a hangover," it says, "is to avoid heavy drinking." (THIS JUST IN: SOCIETY FOR NEEDLESS PODIATRIC INJURY CLAIMS NOT SHOOTING YOURSELF IN THE FOOT RESULTS IN HEALTHIER FEET.) The dictionary goes on to thrash the obvious, telling you to take aspirin and antacids.

But there is one sure-fire cure in the dictionary. It's not listed under hangover, but it can be found in the entry that precedes "hangover." It's called "hanging." I do not recommend this. The noise and effort involved in building your own scaffold is enough to make you wish you were dead.

Thin Metal Tubes
of Certain Death

I PUT THE LUGGAGE IN THE CAR, CHECKED THE TICKETS, and drove to the airport, hands trembling. My wife, aware of how much I hate flying, told me not to worry; this would be over in no time. We'd have a drink before the flight if it made me feel better. Besides, she pointed out, *she* was taking the flight, not me.

Notice: If you are flying soon, do not read any farther, or you will not only cancel your reservations but sit around the house in cement boots, an anvil in your lap, chained to a radiator. If you must read on, console yourself with the knowledge that I am a crank. I hate airplanes. I regard airports as morgues with gift shops. As much as my brain knows the facts on flying—i.e., it's safer than doing some welding while standing up to your knees in gasoline—my heart knows that as soon as *I* get on a plane, it will erupt in flames for no good reason and I will be paste on the landscape.

The rest of my family does not share in this belief. The stewardess could lead my wife to a seat on the wing held down with masking tape, and my wife wouldn't care. My father has a little plane of his own, powered by an engine that can be drowned out by a lawn mower. His interest in flying puzzles me, since duties while a Navy man in the Big

One included knocking planes out of the sky. Proof, I guess, that there is no word in the Lutheran religion for "karma." My father-in-law flies his own plane as well—which I don't understand at all, given that he was shot down while flying in a foreign land a few decades ago. Yes, I know: get back on the horse after you've fallen off. But if the horse *exploded*, I'd get used to walking.

The last plane I took was a DC-10. That's not unusual; the last plane a *lot* of people take is a DC-10. I was back in the Smoking, Nail-Chewing, and Shouting at the Stewardess for Another Scotch, Dammit! Section, listening to Mahler's Fourth on the headsets. Just at the start of the second movement, which the program described as "Death tunes his fiddle," we hit turbulence. Bad turbulence. My stomach did the yo-yo, bounding from feet to gullet, and I decided to get up and hide in the bathroom.

If it's really bad, you see, a sign comes on in the bathroom: RETURN TO SEAT. Meaning, of course, IS THIS WHERE YOU WANT THEM TO FIND YOUR REMAINS? Then I remembered the statistic that fearful fliers always clutch to their heaving bosoms: *more accidents happen in the bathroom than on airplanes*. There was nowhere safe to go. I sat paralyzed. Then the plane began to fall. For ten long minutes, it went down. There was a horrible screech and a jolt.

I thought we'd crashed. Actually, we'd landed.

I was reminded of this flight the other day, when I came across this headline: AIRPLANE DIVES 25,000 FEET. This, I understand, is bad, particularly if you're cruising at 24,999 feet. As I read on, I discovered that the plane did not actually crash. It merely lost cabin pressure. The pilot put the plane into a steep dive until he reached an altitude of 10,000 feet, where no pressurization is needed, although you *still* can't get out and walk the rest of the way.

These things happen, they tell me. Airplanes are still safer than cars. And I have to agree: many is the time when I'm driving along, and the air suddenly becomes unbreathable in my car, and I have to put the car into a steep dive, while dinner trays, magazines, and suitbags fly around the interior of the car. What I find reprehensible about this incident is that *no one told the passengers why they were hurtling to what appeared to be their deaths*. The captain did not use the intercom to say, "That ol' ground sure does look happy to see us, doesn't it just? Don't worry now—jes a li'l ole patch of gravity. Incidentally, y'all might want to make up a will."

Nor did anyone tell them what had happened once it was over. There is a happy ending, however: the plane landed thirteen minutes ahead of schedule. Which explains why this particular airline has such a good on-time record: having to make all the other planes wait because their plane is screaming toward the earth does wonders for the average.

The FAA classified the incident as an "occurrence," which is the least serious of three categories of airplane mishaps. I'm guessing the other two are "plane turned into a convertible in mid-flight but still landed," and "needed a tweezers to find all the parts."

Events like this convince me that flying is not wise. But my wife continues to fly, and I worry about her. Whenever she leaves, I'm convinced I'll never see her again, and I give her a kiss more appropriate for, say, V-E Day. She says that one day I'll have to get up in a plane again, and I say I will. Someday. When hang gliders are accepted as carry-on baggage I'll give the matter some thought.

Why Women Think Men Are Blithering Idiots

<hr>

I'M SURE YOU'VE SEEN THE RECENT SURVEY IN WHICH 73 percent of all women agreed that men are, as a rule, as appealing as garden slugs, although generally better with power tools. Women concurred that men's sole contribution to housework was tracking in the dirt; they found men unable to get emotional about anything that did not contain a great deal of sheet metal, and worst of all, they felt that men regarded women as little more than flank steaks waiting to be slapped on the sizzling grill of their libidos.

Most men's reaction to this has been typical. Most men said, "Yeah? So? Aw, honey, you're not *mad,* are you?" The Men's Rights group—the guys who drive Volvos into the woods, don wolf heads, sit around the fire and get in touch with the nurturing pillager within—these guys whined a little more than usual. The hard-core male chauvinists, the let-me-adjust-my-johnson-while-I-tell-you-what-them-libbers-need types took it as more propaganda from the radical fringe.

I found the survey predictable, and hardly worthy of the attention it's received. Women find fault with men? My God, stop the presses, remake page one. Fact is, men and women have been carping at each other since the Garden of Eden.

After Adam and Eve had eaten the apple and were aware that they were naked—one of the high points in human development, I might add—they had to clothe themselves and vacate the garden. You know and I know that Eve turned to Adam, pointed to the ugly foliage he was wearing, and said, "You're not going out in that, are you?" And you can bet Adam stood around the gate of the garden for five hours, waiting for Eve to get ready. This all goes back a long, long way, folks.

Women have a point on most of the issues, however. Take housework. When I was a bachelor, I never did the dishes. Only when I was kept awake nights when the rapid mold growth made the plates clank in the sink did I wash them. Floors? I'd wait until the dust balls got big enough, then just kick them out the door. Women, however, seem to believe that every surface in a house has to be sterile, in case she suddenly wishes to get up on the mantelpiece and give birth. I suspect this is why women are so happy to be pregnant: after living with a man, they are guaranteed a few hours in a room that is absolutely clean.

Why this is, I don't know. It may be that a girl spends her childhood learning useful skills from her mother, and a boy spends his youth out back with a glove, standing forty feet away from his father while Dad throws hard baseballs at his head. Most men couldn't darn a sock if their very life hung in the balance, but if the sock was thrown at them at high velocity, they could show some hustle and get in front of it.

As for complaints that men always look at women in a sexual way, well . . . sometimes, yes. I don't know how this happens. I don't recall my father shouting, "BY THE WAY, ALL WOMEN ARE SEX OBJECTS," between grounders. I was brought up to respect women and act like a civilized, rational being. I neither leer, nor pinch, nor whistle. But when I met my wife for the first time, I confess that I did not look upon her as someone who might, say, cast new light on my understanding of the Treaty of Ghent. This was wrong, I realize. Aerial spraying of all neighborhoods with saltpeter must begin immediately.

Let's agree that each sex has great gaps in its understanding of the other. Men, for example, will never understand why women need 4,290 pairs of shoes, half of which go with an outfit that is still in the theoretical stage in the mind of some designer. Men won't understand why women eat lunches that look like an overhead perspective of the rain forest, and women won't realize that the reflective coating on microwave pizza trays is an excellent source of zinc. Men will never know what it's like to suffer physical travails once a month, and women will never know what it's like to get hit with a fast grounder right *there*. And then watch your dad try not to laugh.

Recent surveys of men, incidentally, revealed that 100 percent of men agreed with the statement "Women: can't live with 'em," and an equal amount agreed with "can't live without 'em."

If we were more emotionally mature and forthcoming, of course, we'd go into details.

The Phone Book:
A Review

WHEN I WAS A CHILD I HAD TROUBLE DISTINGUISHING
between the phone book and the family Bible. Both were of
equal heft; both were divided into two sections, although the
phone book put the New Testament on yellow pages. Each
featured miles of tiny type arranged in columns, with plenty
of numbers scattered around. To this day, when I quote
Deuteronomy I feel I should give the chapter, verse, and
area code.

I no longer confuse the two, although curious parallels still
exist. The "A" listing shows twenty-two Adams, who, regrettably, are not matched by a single Eve. While that explains the nine Onans on page 1,275, it makes all the more
mysterious the eighty-two Cains on page 244, or the fifty
Abels on page 7. (Eighty-two against fifty—the odds are *still*
bad.)

Given my upbringing, I regard each new phone book as a
scholar of antiquity would welcome a new set of Dead Sea
Scrolls. Of course, a scholar would be skeptical of an ancient
text that was printed in English, arranged alphabetically, and
contained listings for tanning parlors. But I like to regard
the phone book as a means by which future historians will
gauge our culture.

The next such report on the state of St. Paul is not due for a few more months; the 1989–90 phone book appears in June. But over in Minneapolis, where life is lived faster, the 1989–90 phone book is needed sooner. It's been out since January. I finally finished reading it, and I'm here to report on the latest edition.

Just as some enjoy viewing the Good Book as a work of literature, so do I enjoy reading the phone book as a novel. Not since Dickens has a book summed up the people who inhabit a city; not since Joyce has there been so little connection between one line and the next. The prose has a terseness that makes Calvin Coolidge sound like Jerry Lewis on truth serum. Granted, the structure is predictable—when "S" follows "R," the reader sighs, knowing it was bound to happen—but the use of the alphabet to advance the plot reassures the reader. Unlike modern novels that seem to end in mid-story with nothing resolved, the phone book always ends its story at "Z." You're never cheated.

Unfortunately, I regret to note that this year's edition drags. It starts with a spectacular cast of characters in the "A" chapter, then tends to slow down until the last entry in "Z." Let's review some of these highlights.

The first chapter, as always, is a story of human vanity and folly. Everyone seems to want to be the first listing in the phone book, and while many attempt it, few are chosen. One, to be exact. In the last Minneapolis phone book, the first listing was:

A—
MAIN OFFICE
(number.)

Now there's an arresting opening line. It has both mystery and a Kafkaesque sense of menace—Who is A? What do they do? Will there come the day when a strange voice on your answering machine says, "This is A. You have our number," and hangs up?

This year, I am sad to say, the suspense is broken. "A"

—still first—adds that they are "A DBA A-ABC APPLI-ANCE AND HEATING" company, which of course explains everything.

But nothing explains the twelve individuals who go by "A" as their name. Same twelve as last year, although "A" number three, feeling a little less boastful than last year, did not boldface his number in the '89 edition. Why do these people list themselves as merely "A"? Surely they must know that there are eleven other A's in the book, not counting the sinister MAIN OFFICE.

Maybe they don't know they're not the only A in town. I have a vision of them at parties, saying smugly, "Oh, I'm in the book. Just dial A." And then the phone never rings. The receptionist at the MAIN OFFICE has probably had several hundred dates in the last few years, and can't believe his or her luck. "I don't know why, but people keep calling and telling me that they think I'm really interesting and they'd like to go out with me."

Past the one-upmanship of the dueling A's, however, lurk many strange listings. About "A AABLE MASSAGE" we will say nothing. There's four listings for "A-AALL KLEAR," which has a disconcerting, Cold War sound to it; I called them and heard a perky voice say, "All klear," and I felt like saying thanks, I'll get out from under the desk now. "A ABBLE ESCORT SERVICE" exists perhaps to provide comfort to lonely poor spellers. "A BAD GIRL" sounds troublesome, but is far preferable to "A OBNOX-IOUS GIRL," which is a little farther down the page. For those of you with ecumenical tastes, there's "A BRUNETTE BLOND & REDHEAD," but don't blame us if you have to call "A BUG BUSTER EXTERMINATING" afterwards.

If you can't get a spot with one "A," the theory seems to be, then pile on the "A"s and hope someone notices. Page 2 features "A-A-A ABBOTT PLUMBING," perhaps the only plumbing firm staffed by professional Lou Costello impersonators. The four-"A" barrier is broken by a dental clinic, which makes it sound like a howl of pain, and followed

up by "A A A A SANTA CLAUS SUIT AND RENTAL."
And no, that's not pronounced like you think; it means "For
(four) A Santa Claus Suit." But that doesn't help us one
whit when we consider "A-A-A-A-A OIL COMPANY" on
page 5. All one can say is *slow down, collect your thoughts,
don't be nervous, try it again.*

After that, however, the action pales. Multiple "A"s seem
to be legitimate from this point on. Which doesn't mean
interesting characters don't appear from time to time. Page
5 features the "ABRASIVE GROUP," who seem to be at
every party I attend, and page 29 features two listings for
the resigned and somewhat bitter "ALMOST A WIFE."
After that there is an unending profusion of Andersons and
Andersens, and while the chapter closes with a flurry of
AZZ's, it cannot revive our flagging interest. The reader is
compelled to skip ahead.

Tarry, if you might, on the R's, for there are the things
you can Rent. You can rent a Center, a Phone, a Piano, a
Stork, a Tan, a Wreck, a Yacht. One listing throws up his
hands and confesses you are free to "RENT ABOUT ANY-
THING." As for what you can do upon renting, there are
two options: "RENT-N-RUN" and "RENT-N-TRAVEL."
Run if you please, but they'll get you eventually. "Sure, I
can describe him, officer. He was driving a wreck, towing a
yacht, tanned, holding a stork, and talkin' on the phone."

The brief interlude of commerce is not enough to hold our
attention, however, and we move on to the Z's. There is
never any question as to who holds the last entry in the phone
book; it goes each year to the "ZZZZYZZERRIFIC FUN-
LINE." Those Z's are stacked up like locks on a door, barring the blows of the intruder. No one will get past this guy.
I called this number one night, years ago, and found a tape-
recorded message. It was the merry observations of a blind
man, telling us what he'd done lately. The latest message,
which I called just last night, announced the results of a poll
asking the callers which topics they preferred: (*a*) the creative
uses of ambiguity in the arts, or (*b*) a lot of talk about nasal
residue?

Nasal residue won, he said.

It's a long trip from A to Z—from the cool abstraction of the MAIN OFFICE to frank discussion of a stranger's nose—but in between rests the diversity of this community. Everyone with a phone has an entry here; even the numberless Smiths have a line of their own. The phone book stands as a refutation of solipsism, that school of thought that believes the external word to be a product of our imagination. I don't care how good your imagination, it could never come up with "A-A-A-A-A OIL COMPANY." It has no reason to. The book is, in short, enough to make you believe in a Higher Power.

And is this Higher Power merciful? No. You don't believe me? Look at this bill—charges for seventeen directory-assistance calls. Doesn't the Higher Power know that the phone book is a piece of literature—meaning, naturally, that it's something you discuss, not something you actually *read*?

How to Get Big

FREE WEIGHTS OFTEN GET SHORT SHRIFT IN THE FITNESS
pages of newspapers. There are several good reasons. Free
weights don't do much for your heart. They require discipline
and time. Most importantly, the fitness goals of most people
are "lose weight, increase endurance," not "lift piano, drive
head through sheet metal."

But at any decent gym, it's the weight lifters who dominate,
not the tired masses wheezing away on the stationary bikes.
The lifters look huge and strong, and if not everyone wants
to attain their level of bulk, most worry that without *some*
muscle, this whole fitness thing is pointless.

Or so I used to think. A couple of years ago, I spent every
day at the gym, striving for that toned physique that says,
"I have a lot of time on my hands." When I stopped going
to the gym, I began to feel myself shrinking. It was a weight
lifter's worst nightmare: my shirts fit again.

Recently I resumed lifting; it's going slow. At this rate it
will be a year before I have that just-out-of-San-Quentin
look. But it's as much fun as it ever was, and I recommend
it to all. If you worry that you don't know how to behave in
the free-weight section of your gym, take the following
pointers.

SPECIAL EQUIPMENT. Get a big leather belt; it helps to keep your innards from rupturing. (Although rupturing innards are a point of pride among lifters; the favorite phrase around the weight room is not "Go for the burn" but "Go for the exploding intestinal cavity.") Gloves keep you from getting calluses, so you might want a pair. Then again, if a totalitarian regime ever comes into power and decides to liquidate the intellectuals, those calluses might come in handy. "See! Working class! Really!" Your call.

GRUNTING. Making loud, tortured sounds is part of the fun. When lifting, you should mimic the sound of someone speared with a lance and knocked off his horse: a sharp howl of agony as you lift the weight, followed by a noisy exhalation of breath as you set it down (Note: shouting in pain is not permitted if you are using a weight under fifty-five pounds.) With lesser weights, try grimacing as you lift, and hissing like a tractor tire impaled with a crowbar as you bring the weight down.

IRON *VS*. PLASTIC. Some of the tonier clubs have weights coated with plastic; the grim, serious clubs have clanking sets of weights that rattle when you lift them. Avoid the plastic-coated weights; they make no sound when you bang them together. Real weight lifting sounds like two Model A cars making love.

SHOULD I SQUAT? In any gym, you will see people squatting down and hoisting huge barbells, their faces looking as though they are attempting to pass the Manhattan White Pages through their digestive tract. Not recommended. If you look closely, you can see the spots in the mirror where squatters' kneecaps have actually shot out of their legs and cracked the glass.

WORKING IN. Given that most health clubs sell 4,000 memberships per square inch of club space, it is likely that someone will want to use the weight you are using. If this is the case, you can "work in," or take turns using the weights. I advise against it.

This is what usually happens: I'm doing bicep curls. After two exhausting sets, Man-Mountain Wochowksi bounds up and asks to work in. You can no more say, "Hey, wait until I'm done" than you can say, "My, what pert buttocks we have." Man-Mountain then slams through ten pinky-toe curls and drops the weights, gesturing for me to resume. I'm not ready, but I do not want to admit this. I struggle through my set and hand the weights over. Man-Mountain does another set at particle-accelerator speed, then says, "Go ahead." I make it halfway through, then stagger away, blotchy and gasping. Man-Mountain holds me in scorn for the rest of my membership at the gym.

LEARN YOUR LINGO. "Getting large" is adding muscle, preferably enough to constitute a separate human being. "Getting cut" refers to adding enough muscle so that individual muscles poke out, and people can say, "Nice delts" or "Cool lats" or "Assertive, yet nuanced quadroceps." "Getting ripped" is when you have no subcutaneous fat whatsoever, just drum-tight skin over muscle. These are the people who model for med-school classes on the circulatory system.

UNDERSTAND WHY YOU ARE DOING THIS. Most people are not thrilled by massive muscles. The fact that my wife does not have the build of Arnold Schwarzenegger was a large factor in our courtship. But conversely, most people feel more attractive when they have muscles. This leads to the spectacle of several dozen men dripping with sweat, smelling like goats, wearing faded T-shirts from a liquor company, convinced they are irresistible.

Here's the problem. You look your best when you're working out; your muscles fill with blood, swell to abnormal sizes, and make you look like Popeye. But a hip, *fabulous* Popeye. Trouble is, by the time you've showered and headed back into the world, you've deflated.

But trust me. Those thirty seconds you spend walking from the workout room to the showers, when you pass all the people heading off to their workout—you feel like a deity. You are a Weight Lifter, and everyone knows it.

Just don't walk too fast. Hard on the heart, you know.

Backroads Zen

DRIVING THROUGH THE MIDWEST BY FREEWAY IS LIKE listening to a dial tone for eight hours. On the freeway, every mile looks like the last. Every bridge over the road says COUNTY HH on it. Every billboard touts a motel or a fast-food joint. Every time you round a bend, it's like walking through a door into a room that's just like the one you left. No towering redwoods, no mountain ranges shouldering their way into the sky. We have plains, which is scenery flat on its back. Sure, it's uncomplicated, requires little effort. You could say the same thing about a coma.

I've a simple rule: the worse the road, the more interesting the destination. Highways take you to places that are flat and smooth and well-lit, theme parks for the present tense. If you want to hear the old voices, drive on a road that lets you add your shadow to those that have been gathering for years. Take the back roads.

There are no towns on the interstate, only exits. Super-highways keep their distance from the small town, like someone crossing the street to avoid the strange dog on a sagging porch.

It's the state highways that tie the towns together, running

89

from one to another like a friend with news to tell. They run straight through the center of town, and they're not ashamed to pause for a stop light. If the superhighways are straitlaced G-men, these roads are gossipy relatives, with a different change of clothes for every town they visit.

And there are thousands of towns. Unincorporated hamlets with twenty houses, a wooden church, and a boarded-up store; tired towns with a seed merchant, a gas station, a brick church with a fenced-off boneyard. The places where you never see anyone in the yard, on the meager patch of sidewalk along the highway. You wonder if the people disappear when a car comes by, that no one from outside of town ever sees the inhabitants. Occasionally you'll spy a cable dish in a yard, but instead of looking like a means of connecting with the world, the message is still secretive: Leave the world on the porch, please. I'll take it in when you've left.

Some of the towns are large enough to want to get bigger, cities pecking their way out of the shell. You never heard of them, can't enter without feeling like you've stumbled on a lost but still thriving civilization. On the map, it may rate the type size that means "has living residents." Drive through it and you're surprised to see a city large enough to make the hometown kids come back when they're done with college. A tidy community: schools, a clinic, a mall. Broad new streets on the edge of town, ready for the franchises, strip malls, and other embassies of homogeneity to fill them up with the tatty clatter of commerce. One of everything. Someday, two.

Towns like this are the exception. Most of the towns on the back roads aren't going anywhere. I won't give names, as I don't want anyone from Bum Wrist (pop. 3) writing in to say that any fool should know it's the Soybean Capital of Central Southwestern Minnesota, home to Great Soy Days (Aug. 13–14). But I drove through towns that had lain down and never gotten up again, towns that flourished enough to make the current disrepair look pathetic, sad. There'd be a bank on a street corner, a sign flashing the time and temperature like an idle man flipping a coin in the air to keep himself amused. No stoplights in these towns—just a feeble yellow light strung across the intersection.

You can make up stories as you drive through these towns—who founded them, the lives of the men whose names are carved on the cornices of the empty buildings. Whether or not the town had a parade after the war, who lived in the apartments above the drugstore. Who was the first to notice that no one had built anything new in some time, or that there were less children on the street than ten years ago.

When all the towns between the big city and its farthest satellites empty out, when the elderly folk in the faded homes are borne to the churchyard and remanded to the earth, these places will still be here. In these towns, there's not only no one here to build things up, there's no one to tear it down. It works that way for any city, of course; it never dies in a day. People leave, mortar fails. In fifty years, you realize, this road will be lined with ghosts. Town after town made up of dark houses and shuttered stores, the sightless eye of a traffic signal staring over empty intersections.

The back roads, in other words, are not quaint. There's life and death in the usual doses. Boredom, small carnage. Two hours of driving, for example, gave me a windshield opaque with splattered bugs. Some were rather gruesome— one insect that appeared to be made entirely of dijon mustard exploded out of reach of the wipers and I had to put my visor down to block the sight of it. Most of the bugs are evaporated upon impact, which is probably for the best—you don't want to look out at scores of mashed insect faces, all staring in at you. You'd get out every five minutes and scrub the window clean, and you probably wouldn't sleep well for days.

Then there's the casualties on the road, mangled things you try not to hit. There's more of them on the country roads. On superhighways, there seems to be a great barrier between the land and the road, a fence of wind and noise that turns animals away. On the back roads, the highway is simply hard, quiet earth. Until something appears with no warning.

I can understand how birds and woodchucks get hit, but not the deer. Perhaps it's because stupid things scurry at the slightest provocation, and deer, while smart enough to be intrigued by cars, are not high enough on the evolutionary staircase to get out of the way. On my last trip by back roads I saw two young deer dead on the roads; in both cases they lay on the shoulder, legs curled as though leaping, their heads pointing to the woods at the edge of the fields. I pulled off the road when I saw the first one. Looked around. No skid marks. A handful of broken glass glinting in the sunshine as though it had repossessed the light in the deer's eyes. There weren't any flies—yet. Who ever had hit it wasn't far down the road.

Unless you're there when it happens, you can't see why it should happen at all. You arrive late, see something that manages to be beautiful even in death, and you can't think of a reason for it. It happened the next day on a different road; I passed a deer laid out exactly as the first one. There was nothing to be learned by stopping.

Of course, you risk your own life on these roads. You can't pass anyone on a two lane highway without contemplating death—brought, in this case, not by the Grim Reaper but by a withered Swede in a Nash Rambler who will suddenly appear, heading straight toward you.

This is the only caveat of back roads. People drive slow. They cannot be hurried. Half of them, I swear, wait at the intersections with radar guns—they check your speed, note that it is twenty mph above what they plan to drive, then trundle out in front of you. After a while, you have a conga line of ten or more cars, each breathing murder toward the car in front of him, each swerving out in turn to see what idiot is to blame for this.

The real villain is not the person going slow; it's the one behind him, the guy who refuses to pass. The roads twist and double back, with double yellow lines appearing more often than not. When you get a straight road, a clear shot for passing, you've usually enough time to pass one car. Not two.

I had been behind the semi and the pickup for half an hour, grinding my molars down to dust. It had taken me twenty minutes to pass six cars, and now I was stuck here. The pickup hugged the semi close; there was no leapfrogging him. Then came the blessed straightaway. I swung out of my lane, passed the pickup and drew up on the semi. It was as long as a city block. I floored it.

I flooded it. The engine sank like a fat man stepping into wet cement. At this moment a car appeared ahead, grille winking in the sun like a jouster's lance. I pumped the pedal to revive the car, but I was just keeping even with the semi now; there was no hope of passing it. Or of slipping between the semi and truck; they lumbered along like circus elephants, trunk and tail in a tight grip. The car ahead sounded its horn. The semi gave a long rattling blast. *Thanks, guys. I'd have been content to sit here and play toothpick-and-olive with the steering column if you hadn't warned me.* I braked. There was enough juice left over to get back into my lane.

Oh, but there's more. The car stalled when I tried to give it more gas, and I had to pull off the road and let it have its snit. Every car I'd passed in the last half hour sped by while I stood there like a recruiting officer for impotence.

Well, so what's my hurry? I thought. You want to get somewhere fast, take the big wide road. You wanted to see the backlands, here they are. Breathe deep and look around.

That was when the trip started to be a pleasure. After the car was running again, I found a town that wasn't on the map. I turned onto a side street—I had a choice of two—and took it deep into the fields. I was lost, until it petered out into gravel and dead-ended. Then I turned around and tried to retrace my steps by memory. The map was of no use whatsoever, and that, I realized, was the way I wanted it to be.

Bloody Movies

I'VE SEEN ONLY TWO MOVIES THIS SUMMER, AND ALREADY I've watched about 15,000 people die. Now, I enjoy a good shoot-'em-up as much as the next glassy-eyed, socially maladjusted drifter, but the level of violence in movies is getting so baroque that I leave each movie feeling like I qualify for the Witness Protection Program.

Example. *Total Recall,* a movie starring That Lovable Hun, Arnold Schwarzenegger. As usual, the bad guys cannot hit Arnold, who is quite literally the broad side of a barn, and so they content themselves with liquefying the bystanders. By the time the first half of the movie is over, most of North America looks like it was vigorously rubbed up against a cheese grater.

And these are not tidy deaths. It's not like the old days of gunshot wounds. In the '40s, for example, when a guy took a slug from a roscoe, he grimaced, clutched his stomach as though troubled by a sharp pang of wind, and fell forward. In the westerns, good guys were only shot in the shoulder, a wound that could be cured simply by grabbing at the affected area and tightening the muscles of the jaw. In the movies of the '50s, few died of gunshot—they were stabbed by reefer-crazed juvenile delinquents, which made their eyes go wide for a few seconds; then they crumpled balletically to the sound of rapidly struck bongos.

In the '60s, all the good guys—i.e., criminals who were simply misunderstood rebels—died in slow motion, cut down by the pigs and the Establishment, *man.* Remember *Bonnie and Clyde,* starring Faye Dunaway and Dick Tracy—Bonnie did the Winchester Twist in the front seat of that car for about an hour and a half. This was the age of Poetic Violence, heavily influenced by a long-running piece of performance art called the Vietnam.

No more these gentle deaths. Nowadays it's not a real movie if a gunshot doesn't lift someone off their feet and hurl them through a plate-glass window thirty blocks away. A gunshot wound in these movies is actually the quickest way across town.

Listen, fellas: it's not necessary. I happen to like Arnold Schwarzenegger, but not because he kills fifty people a minute. I find the *RoboCop* movies entertaining, but *not* because of the spattering viscera. I look at these movies like a pet owner looks at his cat when he brings dead birds to the door. *I know this is your way of showing you care, but it's really not required.*

Death, in some form or another, hangs over every movie made this summer. *Ghost Dad,* starring Bill Cosby, asks the pressing question: What if Bill Cosby were made largely of ectoplasm? The trailer for *Exorcist III* begins with a priest going bum-over-teakettle down a flight of stone stairs, and after that it's all damnation and gouts of pea soup. *Die Hard 2: Die So Hard the Mortician Has to Use a Chisel* concerns terrorists who take over an airport, so presumably there will be plenty of barking gats and ruptured tourists.

I'm not certain what this means. It might be that directors use constant gunfire so as not to overuse any of the seven or eight words that make up most movie dialogue. It might be that we are jaded, that the death of one means nothing, but the death of half of the membership of Actors Equity really makes our weekend.

Who knows. Better, I suppose, that we have our murderous, carnal, triple-dipped-in-id impulses played out on the screen. If it weren't for these movies, we'd probably invade Canada, just to see some action. I just worry that every damn movie is going to be this way. They're talking, for example, about making a movie out of Curious George, the gentle, mischievous monkey who hangs around with the man in the big yellow hat. (No, not Dick Tracy.) I hate to see what they'll do with kind little George.

I can guess. Terrorists will burst in, kill the man in the big yellow hat. Curious George will be taken to a secret lab, be subjected to experiments. (Lots of close-ups of needles, electrodes, dental picks.) Through an accident, George is exposed to a radioactive isotope that makes him invincible and he breaks free and kills everyone in the Western Hemisphere who deserves it. *Furious* George. The sequel? Easy. A duel to the death with Winnie the Pooh.

Microbe Liberation

EVERY TIME I SEE A BUMPERSTICKER THAT READS "FUR IS dead," I always have the same thought: I SHOULD CERTAINLY HOPE SO. Being dead is one of fur's strongest selling points. When I drape my coat over a chair, I do not want to keep checking to see if it has slithered off and is dragging itself toward the door. Nor do I want to get care and cleaning instructions that say, "If FUR shows signs of life, put it in the garage with the motor running for several hours. Then dry clean."

Not that I have a fur coat. I can't afford one, and I don't want one. Given my height, I would look silly in one, much like a large dog taught to walk on its back legs. People would look for a hat to throw money into. And there is something vaguely barbaric about ripping off the skin of one species for self-adornment of another, but I can't get too high and mighty about that; if spandex came from something living, I'd bait the traps and hone the knives.

It's the people who *do* get high and mighty that perturb me. I can understand having strong feelings about the issue. But according to *New York* magazine, anti-fur activists have recently torched a California fur store, shot out the windows of one N.Y.C. store, and painted MURDERER on the pavement in front of another. Any day now, some furrier is going to take a midnight stroll to the bathroom and step into a leg trap. Given the proclivity of the trapped animal to chew its leg off in order to escape, I predict that by the year 2000, over half of the nation's furriers will be known by the nickname "Peg Leg."

The cause, I'll admit, is just; treatment of fur-bearing animals can be appalling, and I can see no reason why animals should be made to feel horrible pain so that someone can rub its pelt in their face and feel pampered. But the extremists of the anti-fur movement view the wearing of fur as a crime justifying the reconvening of the Nuremberg trials. The *New York* magazine article even cited a banner that read "World Peace Begins with Your Wardrobe," as though thermonuclear war could erupt over clashing plaids.

The extreme anti-fur crowd shares certain sentiments with the fringes of the animal-rights people. According to their view, animals and humans are, by virtue of being alive, equal. I don't agree. I don't feel it is my God-given right to shine my boots on the hindquarters of any handy quadruped, just because I'm bigger and can speak in complex sentences. But just because something is alive does not mean it is my equal, or that it deserves my respect. When I see a silverfish scuttling across the basement floor, "Hail, Comrade" is not the first thought that comes to mind. I don't let mosquitoes land on my arm, tap a vein, and bloat themselves until they stagger off like winged tennis balls; I kill them, I curse them, and smile when I do so. Sometimes I swat flies *just because.*

Ah, well, you say, those are insects. They don't count. Really? Why not? Isn't everything that lives entitled to equal treatment? Who are we to say that Beethoven was greater than the mold on his cheese?

The more I think about it, the more I realize that the hardcore animal-rights crowd doesn't go far enough. They only concern themselves with the cute species—the sniffling bunnies, the wet-eyed calves, the laughing dolphins. If it doesn't remind them of a Smurf, they can't be bothered. It's time that someone stood up for the life forms with brains the size of pencil points. (Politicians are excluded; they have reelection committees to look after their interests.)

I hereby declare the following Popular Fronts to look after the interests of neglected species.

The Parasite Anti-Defamation League. Our slogan: "World Peace Begins in Your Upper Intestine." Parasites give us a lesson in interdependence, in mutual trust and cooperation. Drink from a stagnant pond in rural Mexico *today*.

Society for the Preservation of Boll Weevils. Our slogan: "Weevils Died For Your Sweater." Since the harvesting of cotton deprives the boll weevil of its food, all cotton fabrics are to be opposed. The politically correct person wears only polyester.

Save the Dust Mites. Our slogan: "Brooms = Genocide." Since there are several billion mites in any given household, the American habit of cleaning and sweeping murders billions of helpless mites, often through chemical warfare. Stop the slaughter; stay thy dustmitt.

The Coalition to Save the Leech. Our slogan: "Give Blood." Since the wetlands of the world are vanishing at an alarming rate, the humble leech faces a loss of its livelihood. Yet every human being continues to use his own blood for his own selfish purposes.

If all goes well, these organizations will catch on, and we will all be respectful of our fellow creatures. Humans will no longer adorn themselves with the skin of other beings, or eat them for sustenance. We can survive on beans and lettuce.

They may be life forms, but we are permitted to use them as we see fit. If God had meant us to spare them, he would have given them big eyes with which to look up at us.

The CIA Entrance Exam

AND NOW, A QUIZ.

1. You are a secret agent for the CIA. Mexico has just elected a Communist government whose first action in power is to line its northern border with mobile, nuclear-tipped missiles. What do you do?
A) Blame Congress.
B) Convene Congress, then penny the doors shut and nuke Mexico.
C) Assassinate the entire Mexican government by inviting it to a picnic and serving potato salad that has been kept in the trunk all afternoon.

2. You are a secret agent for the CIA. Your contact in Moscow has just learned that the U.S.S.R. is planning a full-scale strike against the United States for no apparent reason. What do you do?
A) Call Vegas for the line.
B) Mutter "Men!" and stamp out of the room.
C) Get a steely, ruthless look in your eye and put a James Bond movie soundtrack on the stereo.

3. You are a secret agent for the CIA. A Communist agent contacts you, says he wants to defect, and asks you to help him over the Berlin Wall. What do you do?

A) Spend all week buying back the pieces of the Berlin Wall and hastily rebuilding it over the weekend.

B) Try and dissuade him from defecting by citing the inflated housing market.

C) Bring a ladder and pretend you are scaling and descending a wall; it's the least you can do.

The answers? Don't ask me. I'm a civilian. I know nothing of the CIA. I know that it does some questionable things, some nasty things, and some absolutely necessary things, like spy on the Sovs. And yes, I know that the spying on the Sovs is a tired hangover of the Cold War mentality now that Gorby delivers the KGB's "Things to Do Today" list to the White House. Until they are the fifty-first state, however, I want to know if they have a space-based laser aimed at my house, so I can move my car.

I said I know nothing of the CIA, but that's not exactly true. My ignorance has been ameliorated by a revealing new book called *The CIA Entrance Examination,* yours from Simon and Schuster. Written by John Patrick Quirk, president and publisher of the Foreign Intelligence Press, it's for people who want a career in the CIA..

Each section makes for enjoyable, if blood-chilling, reading. Such as:

ABOUT THE CIA. This section begins with a discussion of the CIA's history, including a revealing passage called "What the CIA Really Does." (Like they're going to tell you.)

"Man has been engaged in intelligence activities . . . from time immemorial," the book notes. "The Old Testament tells us of the Lord instructing Moses to round up 'three men, that they may search the land of Canaan, and that Moses sent twelve men to spy out the land.' " One of the apocryphal texts has Moses sending the twelve men to "scope out the chicks," leading one to question the translation of "land of milk and honey," but never mind; point is, spies have always been with us. The Old Testament, the book might have noted, also tells us of Satan coming in the guise of a snake and making a double agent of Eve. And there was Lucifer's defection, even earlier.

But this only goes so far. If the CIA had been present at Creation, the Bible would have withheld the actions of the last five days, and half the Bible would be available on a "need-to-know basis."

"In 1775," the book says, skipping right ahead, "the second Continental Congress established the first American intelligence organizations with the creation of the Secret Committee and then the Committee of Secret Correspondence."

Translation: we were here before the Constitution, so when it comes to the moral high ground, we have squatter's rights.

According to my research, both agencies set the pace for subsequent CIA activity. The first thing they did was to establish a series of Latin American governments and promptly overthrow them, just for practice. The Secret Committee also, in a foretaste of the U-2 missions, attempted flyover spy missions of Cuba by getting a good running start, leaping high in the air off Florida, and quickly sketching anything they happened to see.

The Secret Committee was skilled at stamping out all revolutionary activity until Congress took it aside and explained that they *were* the revolutionaries.

The precursor of today's CIA was the OSS, a wartime intelligence operation that told Gregory Peck where the Guns of Navarone were. After that, it became the CIA, mainly because the OSS had used up its entire yearly allotment of pushpins and could get more by becoming a brand-new government agency.

HOW TO APPLY TO THE CIA. Let's say you get a call, saying that the agency recruiters were impressed by your résumé, in particular the way it had been treated with a chemical that made everyone who handled it subject to violent hallucinations for three days. You show promise. They want to interview you next week.

Here's where it gets downright sinister.

"The interviewer," the book says, "who is probably an old and trusted operator in the intelligence game, asks the questions, and you do the answering."

Am I alone in feeling the breeze of a swinging rubber hose in that statement? Read on: "The session is often pleasant, and only unpleasant if you make it so."

Hint, hint.

"At some stage," the section concludes, "you take an intelligence aptitude test, and then you wait . . . and wait some more."

I hope they bring you food and water.

THE APPLICATION. The book gives a sample of what to expect in the written exam—100 questions on everything from your credit rating to your opinion of the Reykjavik summit. And there's no bluffing it like you did in high school when you didn't know the answer:

"The summit was held on Reykjavik, which is a large city in Iceland. Iceland is actually not full of ice; that is more accurately a description of Greenland. Iceland gets most of its energy from geothermal sources, which provide summits with plenty of heat. Chief exports include wool, inconclusive arms treaties."

There are maps on which you have to locate countries, identify alliances, and color in certain nations. (Until recently, applicants for the KGB entrance exam were promoted for coloring outside the lines and as far into neighboring countries as possible.) Telling your interviewer that "I see Chad in salmon pink, to offset the peach shadings I've given the Congo" will not do you well. Coloring liberal states like Minnesota or Massachusetts, however, in red or pink almost guarantees your admission.

Here are some real questions, and my recommendations on how *not* to answer them.

Q. Please describe your motivation for choosing a career with the CIA.

A. Interest in national security, pens that squirt cyanide, protecting American interests, hot cars that release oil slicks and have ejector seats, indentifying and containing actions inimicable to national security, hot babes in cocktail dresses. Oh, plus upholding democracy and killing people with little wires through the ear canal.

Q. Would you be able to endure extended periods of time in which you are unable to communicate with family and friends?

A. Sure. I do it every time I go home for Christmas.

Q. How do you feel about living in an area that is politically unstable and potentially violent?

A. See previous answer.

Q. Would you like to live in a war zone?

A. Oh, sure! Paint me in Day-Glo and let me promenade around Cambodia! Dress me up like Custer and drop me in downtown Beirut! I am so sure!

READING COMPREHENSION. The reading section is called "Dropping to Levkovitz." This is not a third-down play from the University of Tel Aviv football playbook. It's a story about a female agent who crawls through a sewer to smuggle a baby to the West, is shot at the border, but makes it to the hospital, where she stays alive long enough to give the baby's identity and destination and then dies.

It is written about someone who used to do the job you're now applying for.

Think about that. If you comprehend that, and you still want the job, you're CIA material. There are, I should tell you, a few details that seem minor but are crucial to the story. For example, the agent, named ████████ is described as wearing a ████████ but when she ████ she is described as ████████████ It's not really ███ at all, so don't be ██████

That I can tell you the secrets of that passage tells you what a free country we live in. Isn't America just wonderful?

Friday the 13th

IT'S FRIDAY THE 13TH. SO WHAT? WHO CARES? I'M NO
slave to arcane and misinformed medieval superstition, and
I never will be, knock on wood. No, on days like today I
delight in walking under ladders, smashing mirrors, opening
umbrellas indoors, spilling sacks of salt until my house looks
like an Antarctic wilderness, buying black cats by the sackful
and drawing lines of sardine paste on my floor so they will
cross my path continuously.

Superstition, in short, is nonsense. Here is a quote on naval
superstition from *Strange Stories, Amazing Facts,* a book of
lore from *Reader's Digest,* aimed squarely at the a-profile-
of-a-weeping-Jesus-has-appeared-on-my-refrigerator set:

"Not only was the ship called the Friday, but its keel was
laid on a Friday, and for good measure, it was commanded
by a captain Friday. The British Admiralty had decided to
expose the absurdity of one of the Royal Navy's most cher-
ished superstitions—that Friday is an unlucky day. Their
plans might well have worked. But on its maiden voyage—
on a Friday—the ship disappeared with all hands. No trace
was ever found."

Interesting story, right? A cautionary tale about man's hubris, or the vagaries of coincidence, or whatever you want to hang on the episode. But there's more:

"The Admiralty has consistently denied that this story is true, but *its denials are unimportant* [my emphasis]. Generations of British seamen have accepted every word of it."

I offer: those are some mighty stupid seamen. Never was there an old briny Limey perched on a barrel of jerky who said "Y'know, mates, given that our entire concept of days and weeks is just one way of representing the passage of this planet through space, and an arbitrary way at that, there's really no cause to say there's anything intrinsically unlucky about Friday."

If such an old salt did exist, they probably would have tossed him overboard. And waited until Friday to do it, so his shipmates could ascribe his disappearance to bad luck.

There are plenty of equally enlightened superstitions in our history. It was believed that you could get luck by touching wood (although nowadays a TV anchorperson suffices). Eggshells were not thrown into the fire because that might offend the hen; apparently slaughtering their menfolk and subjecting the interior of the eggs to gruesome infanticide troubled the hens not a whit. In Malta, churches have two clocks, one to show the correct time, the other to fool the Devil so he will not know when Church really starts. This, of course, assumes that the Devil, an omnipresent and powerful foe who built his entire franchise on the concept of deception, cannot see two clocks, note when people go to church, and *figure it out for himself*. The Devil, I imagine, is the sort of chap who *likes* to be fashionably late, anyway.

Not all superstitions are irrational; some sound like tidy justifications for otherwise questionable behavior. In Ireland, for example, it is considered lucky to spill your drink on the ground; this is nominally a holdover from the old custom of pouring a drink for the gods. But as anyone who has ever encountered Irish liquor can attest, spilling your drink on the ground can be such a frequent occurrence you *need* a superstition to justify your actions. I imagine that in back-woods Appalachian moonshine country, missing the turn and driving your car into a TVA reservoir in the middle of the night is also considered lucky.

Scotland weighs in with this curiosity: it is unlucky to throw vegetables into the fire. Not ever having seen vegetables of Scottish derivation in the stores, I wonder if they have some peculiarly explosive quality. Readers of Scottish papers who regularly see news of good citizens stunned and singed by carelessly tossed leeks are requested to write me with the details. Or maybe I am on the wrong approach; perhaps Scots are trying not to offend the simple barnyard creatures who lay the vegetables.

Consider this gem from Nigeria, courtesy the pithy stylists at *Reader's Digest:* "If a man is hit with a broom, he becomes impotent unless he retaliates seven times with the same broom." Yeah. Sure. Probably paying homage to the God of Tooled Wood, and beating his woman with great reluctance.

It's the appearance of the number seven in disparate cultures that gives the anthropologists pause, and leads to untold theses on the meaning of numbers. Like thirteen, seven has a certain cachet in superstition. There is certainly a reason for that, but the answer is none too enlightening. Every number used to mean something. There were good-luck numbers and bad-luck numbers. Seven is good or bad, depending on where you are in the world and what the previous shooter has just rolled. On the island of Java, where the famous Tribe of the Cross-Eyed reside, the number two, for some reason, is considered holy. The Pilgrims viewed the square root of twenty-two as a sign of unspeakable evil (you could be put in the stocks for calculating pi beyond three digits on a Sunday). Interestingly enough, anthropologists have found that the number one billion means absolutely nothing to people in Washington, D.C.

But thirteen is the champ; thirteen means bad mojo to just about everyone. This goes back—surprise!—to superstition. Although thirteen's role as a harbinger of malfeasance can be traced to the Last Supper (thirteen guests, not counting the waiter), it goes back to pre-Christian times as well. Norse mythology holds that twelve gods were sitting down to a meal when Loki, recognizable to some from the Thor comic books as a horny-headed guy in yellow and green tights, appeared and started a fight. Balder, beloved of the Norse gods because his hair was receding faster than everyone else's, was killed.

So today, millions of people of Norse descent are on guard. Dinner parties are tense. People in gatherings of twelve know that if a guy dressed like a superhero comes in and taunts them about the wine they've chosen, they must stay calm. Especially the ones wearing the toupees.

Even though thirteen is known worldwide for its badness, every number meant one thing or another to the unenlightened masses. The reason is simple: they had no TV. They could not assign channels to those numbers, and had to come up with other connotations. Those of us born in the television age have associations with numbers, all right, but they are the channels of the TV stations with which we grew up. When I think of the number four, for example, I think of a Fargo TV sportscaster who wore painfully festive plaid jackets that were so loud they frequently gave the score before he could. The number six means respectability, for this is the station on which my parents watched the news. Eleven was the number that boasted having the world's highest TV tower. It fell over one year, so when people say *eleven* I instinctively toss twisted pieces of metal and guy wires over my shoulder.

But don't take this as an endorsement of superstition. I'll show you just how brave I am. I met a young woman on Nov. 13, 1987. *Friiiiiday* the 13th, just like the movies say. When I went to pick her up, I was nervous; I can still feel the stiff leather of my new shoes, the bristle of the stems of the roses I clutched, the damp, humid feel of my breath collecting in my hockey mask. But everything went well. So well that we got married.

We didn't have a calendar handy when we set the date;

we thought August, early, after my birthday, on a Sunday. And yes, it turned out to be the 13th of the month.

It was a small ceremony. Twelve people. There would have been more, but her side of the family chartered a bus from Friday Lines. Funny: they set off two days before the wedding, but they never showed up.

Wanted, Debt or Alive

A SOBER INDIVIDUAL WOULD HAVE LOOKED AT A DEAL that put him 10 billion in debt and run shrieking from the room. Robert Campeau, the Canadian financial genius who borrowed $10 billion to buy a chain of American department stores, apparently regarded the deal as though it were one of those record-club ads in the back of magazines. *Get 250 retail stores for a penny! Nothing more to buy ever! Pay only $10 billion shipping and handling!*

Don't blame him. Blame the investors. This type of idiocy was common in the heady days of the boom market; anyone who showed up at a bank not wearing prison stripes and dragging an iron ball was regularly given billions to do with as they saw fit. Bankers developed bulging biceps from the constant exertion of throwing good money after bad. A curious philosophy emerged: if you owe more money than you can possibly pay off, you must be a good credit risk.

I've seen this philosophy at work. Before I bought my house, I had bad credit. I couldn't bum a smoke without collateral. Banks not only returned my credit-card application, but they attached a restraining order. Then I went to the Gotti-Gambini E-Z Credit Co. ("Your place for home

110

loans. Also for cement.'') and I was instantly approved for a mortgage. Nice terms, although every payment is a balloon payment. Meaning, if I don't make it, they blow me up. The point is, I was now heavily indebted, and thus, every banker's friend.

Now a day doesn't go by without a Visa application in my mailbox. If I accepted every offer that came my way and spent the cards to the limit, my financial situation would be Campeauesque in the extreme. So far, I've avoided the temptation, but I worry about debt anyway. In fact, I think of Campeau every time I'm laying in bed, sweating, stiff as a wooden plank, seeing the words UPCOMING MORTGAGE PAYMENT written on the ceiling in fiery, throbbing letters. I wonder how anyone owing $10 billion could sleep. Perhaps Campeau had a butler come in each night and strike him about the head with a hammer to give him a helpful concussion. *Harder, Jeeves, I've a payment due tomorrow.*

But it's not just the insane level of debt that makes this story so pathetic; it's the way in which he amassed his debt. Part of Campeau's financing came from junk bonds—high-yield securities that are usually backed by nothing more than pocket change and a desperate grin. Good bonds have ratings like AAA; junk bonds usually have ratings of DDDD (ad infinitum), which means that they are likely to default while they are being printed. Junk bonds boomed in the '80s, but news of Campeau's financial troubles, according to the January 8th issue of *Newsweek*, "sent the $200 billion junk-bond market into a spin."

Here's an insight into the brilliant minds that rule the financial world: someone had to welsh on $10 billion worth of markers before they realized that "junk bonds" are so named for a particular reason. These are the guys who would order a meal named Death Food and look shocked when they pitched face-forward into the table. In the '80s, however, there was no such thing as a bad bond. Brokers could shout "Hey! Fellahs! Look what I'm selling! Compost Bonds!

111

Make-Sure-You've-Had-Your-Tetanus-Shot Bonds! I'm-Off-To-Rio-As-Soon-As-Your-Check-Clears Bonds!" and the investors would form a line.

If you think the Campeau junk-bond deal was extreme, consider RJR-Nabisco. The marriage of tobacco firm R. J. Reynolds and wafer concern Nabisco—the deal required $25 billion worth of debt. The company said it expected to pay the debt through sales of its new Lower Tar Oreo, but analysts say more work is needed. If the company follows the typical leveraged-buyout strategy, it will pay the debt by cutting costs and selling off portions of the company—exactly what Campeau said he'd do. I wish them luck. I only know that when I told the guy at Gotti-Gambini E-Z Credit that I would pay my mortgage by selling the porch and the kitchen and turning down the thermostat, he gave a curious, humorless laugh, and proceeded to explain how fingers fell into the category of "seizable goods."

Now that I think about it, I think corporations ought to finance their debt through loans from organized crime. Massive debt may indeed force a company to be more productive, but a nail-studded baseball bat also does the job, and at a fraction of the price. Granted, no one wants the beaches of the East Coast to be closed because CEOs keep washing up on the shore. But look at it this way. When Wall Street firms arrange the financing, it results in huge bonuses for guys who go right out and buy a BMW, or a Mercedes. Give the money to the mob, and they'll spend it on heavily armored Lincoln Town Cars. Say what you will about the mob, at least they buy American.

The Talkies

━━━━━━━━━━━━━━━━━━━━━━━━

I AM A TOLERANT MAN. ESPECIALLY AT THE MOVIES. I DO not complain when the seats are as plush as a Baptist pew, or the buttered popcorn tastes like packing material with a drizzle of melted crayon. I don't mind that I have to cash a bond to buy a box of Dots, and if I have to use solvents to free my feet from the floor at the end of the film, that's acceptable. I'm not happy when the man with the big yellow hat from the Curious George books sits directly in front of me and blocks my view, but accept it as the price you pay for a communal experience.

But people who talk in movies make me turn eight shades of mad. Plunk two talkers behind me and I start to pine for a decent billy club. Something well weighted with a comfortable grip. As I see it, there are two excuses for talking during movies: (*a*) you are on the screen; or (*b*) you have a rare neurological disease that causes you to blurt out statements like "I CAN'T BELIEVE SISKEL AND EBERT GAVE THIS TWO THUMBS UP!" at inappropriate times—and so you go to movie theaters where your affliction seems less bizarre.

Mind you, I am not discussing those who lean to their partner and whisper a few words or observations. Most of

113

you whisper, or keep it to yourselves. The people to whom I refer are those who speak at a volume just a few decibels shy of the level you would use to warn someone in a crowd of a falling piano. The people who seem to expect their names to be listed in the credits under "Additional Dialogue."

Last week I went to see *Mississippi Burning*. I use the word "see" with precision, for I heard not a line of the dialogue. The entire row behind me talked all through the trailers. That's fine. That's what trailers are for. Go on, get it out of your system. They also talked during the opening credits, but that was acceptable; they'd arrived late—I know this because one of them hit me in the head with her purse —and they were still flush with the excitement that comes with leaving the house three minutes before the film starts.

But as the film progressed, it became obvious that the row behind us was a group from the Institute for Pointing Out the Obvious, off on a field trip. The first image of the film, an early '60s-model car cresting a hill, prompted the gentleman behind me to note, "That's an old car." The appearance of several more cars of the same period gave the man an empirical Epiphany, and he could not help but burst out with his conclusion:

"This must be set in the past."

There was a period of silence, during which he may or may not have whispered, "Note how reflective and rectangular the screen is," to his partner. The slack was taken up by a group to his right, who were attempting to recall what this film was about, perhaps on the assumption that the plot, due to malicious filmmakers anxious for financial ruin, would remain inscrutable for the next two hours.

These folk soon shut up—after my buddy had turned around, locked eyes, and given his best I-taught-Manson-all-he-knows look. But the ones behind me were just beginning.

Nothing escaped comment. The streets in the rural Mississippi town were unpaved? Lo, hear them discuss the volume of dust raised by a passing car. The sheriff was fat? Lend an ear to "Looka that gut," and other biting witticisms (such as, "I mean it, how can he be that fat? I'll never get that fat."). Woe to any screen characters who fail to heed their judgments, and prolonged approval of those who do.

Often I was treated to a critical evaluation in process. At one point, Gene Hackman drives up to the house of a woman who knows something but isn't telling the Feds. This prompts the following speech:

"Oh, it's broad daylight, he'd better not go up to that house. People would talk and her husband would hear about it, don't you think?"

"I imagine so."

"Well, everyone knows that's his car."

"See, he's leaving."

"Yeah, he's turning around."

"Good. 'Cause he'd have gotten in trouble, and so would she."

Turning around and shouting "SHUT UP! SHUT UP AND REMAIN IN A STATE OF SHUTUPEDNESS!" would have done no good. I had spent the previous hour turning around and glaring, but they apparently took this to mean I was angry that they were speaking too softly, and hence depriving me of their views. For a while I was turning around, glaring and turning away with a heavy sigh, but given the classical decor of the theater, they probably interpreted this as a nostalgic sigh of regret for an idealized world long passed. Nothing worked. When the man issued a few racking coughs interspersed with words, I considered lighting up a cigarette and letting the smoke waft his way, but smoking, of course, is considered discourteous to others.

For a while I attempted to use telekinesis to loose a piece of plaster on the ceiling directly above them, but this did not work.

I finally turned around and said, "Quiet!" They nodded, as though I was describing an attribute of the theater. I might as well have said "Dark!" or "Chairs in rows!" They embarked anew on another discussion of whether or not that actor was in that Jack Nicholson film.

Actors, incidentally, were not allowed to have roles. When

they discussed the motivations of Gene Hackman's character, they addressed him as Gene Hackman. "See, Gene Hackman wants to do it his way, that's the problem." This helped all of us within hearing range maintain our suspension of disbelief. Willem Dafoe, late of *Platoon,* was known only as "the guy in the glasses." They would occasionally bring out the depth in his character by asking, "Why is he always wearing a suit? It looks so warm, doesn't he sweat?"

If I seem to be exaggerating, I assure you I am not. These people babbled without cease, as though the fountain at the concession stand had added sodium pentothal to their beverages. I could not move, as there was not a decent seat to be had in the theater. I could barely concentrate on the film, as I was always steeled for another pronouncement. All I could do was entertain the idea of following them home, standing in the corner of their bedroom, and saying things like, "Oh, see, he has his arm around her shoulder, he likes her. Okay, well, she's getting ready for bed now, that's a nice set of sheets, I have ones like those at home. Say, that's quite a mole, I'd get that checked out if I had a mole like that," and so forth.

It would only be fair.

So, friends, if you're in a movie house, and you have something to say, ask yourself this: Do you, in the course of your day, constantly have to shout over the sound of a jackhammer, and should you now adjust your voice accordingly? Is what you have to say really necessary? Is the gentleman in front of you waving a flag on which is printed the nautical symbol for PUT A LID ON IT?

If you feel you still have to speak, ask yourself this: If this was World War II, and I was behind German lines with Nazis everywhere, could the Nazis hear me if I spoke at this level, and subsequently submit me to horrible torture? If the answer is yes, tone it down. Or write it out and hand it to your partner, with the instructions to swallow it immediately.

Or, go on talking. Go ahead. You paid your money. Gab it up. And make sure you kick the seat in front of you when you cross your legs. You're only conforming to ancient tradition, after all. Movies are nothing more than modern versions of cavemen telling tales around the fire, and back then there were always a couple who talked all through the story.

We know this because of drawings on the walls of caves where they buried the talkers.

Smoke 'Em If You Got 'Em

A TOBACCO COMPANY RECENTLY SAID THEY EXPECTED THE market for cigarettes to shrink in the coming years. They gave no reason. This is like the the National Council for the Promotion of Extremely Slippery Tubs predicting a rise in serious head injuries, but professing ignorance as to the cause. The tobacco companies speak of changing consumer preferences, or diminishing markets—as in, "Uncle Mort, who smoked for forty years, was diminished last Friday at North Memorial Hospital." Whatever they say, they know that by 2000 there will three smokers in America. And two of them will be trying to quit.

There's not too much the tobacco companies can do about it. Going after kids is taboo, which leaves out sponsoring children's books like *Winnie the Pooh Lights Up*. Nor can they come out and encourage people to smoke more—a slogan like "Forty a day, that's all we ask" is probably not going to fly. Instead, the cigarette manufacturers are going to claw at one another, wooing smokers away from competing brands. To achieve this, they're introducing specialty brands aimed at certain slivers of the market.

For example. There was—for about five minutes—a brand called Uptown cigarettes, targeted at blacks. Uptown was a menthol, which many blacks prefer to regular flavor, and the cigarettes were packed upside down, catering to a certain portion of the black market that opens their cigarette packs from the bottom. From the protest that erupted when the brand was announced, you'd have thought they named the things Shiftless Rastus 100s. Uptowns were poleaxed.

Another example of specialty cigarettes is—and I'm not kidding—Harley-Davidson brand. Forgive me if I make any generalizations about Harley riders—I know they all hold Ph.D.s and take their motorcycles to the symphony on the weekends, and on weekdays use their bikes to deliver meals-on-wheels to shut-ins—but I can't help thinking Harley cigarettes will go after the leather-and-tattooed-back crowd. You can imagine the slogan: "For a taste that's tailpipe fresh."

Why stop there? I propose the following specialty cigarettes, based on various markets and products seeking new affiliations. I have provided suggested slogans.

BMW Lights. "Finally. A cigarette with precision German engineering." Leather will line the interior of the package. A carton will cost $432, excluding tax and license. Unfortunately, the package will spend most of its time in the shop, since the hinge on the flip-top box tends to stick.

Nubbins. "For the man who hasn't time to smoke." Nubbins burn down to the filter after one puff, allowing the consumer to chain-smoke more easily.

Nautilus Menthols. "A workout in every puff." Contains 1,000 times the nicotine of ordinary cigarettes; elevates your heart rate to fifty times your resting pulse rate. For the health fanatic who hasn't time to get to the gym.

Panhandler 180s. "They're bum-proof!" Panhandlers are extra long, but they only come one to a pack, so you can honestly tell the bum that you're smoking your last one.

New Yorkers. For readers of *New Yorker* magazine. Slogan: "For the smoker who enjoys a 38-part essay on why 'Tastes Good Like a Cigarette Should' is appalling grammar." New Yorkers are for those who are trying to quit; each week the consumer will intend to get around to smoking them, but will never do more than read the cartoon on the side of the package.

This is just a sample of what you can expect. As with any industry in hard times, it's dog-eat-dog. And how appropriate that metaphor: a cigarette tastes *so* good after a meal. Anyone for Fido 100s?

The Earth Is Not
Our Buddy

━━━━━━━━━━━━━━━━━━━━━━━━━━━━━

WHEN IT COMES TO OUR TREATMENT OF THE PLANET, I doubt we'll get the damage deposit back. In case you've missed all the wretched news, let me summarize.

1. The earth is about a week and a half away from destruction. Scientists are not sure of the causes; some say the weight of discarded disposable diapers will cause the earth to be drawn closer to the sun, heating up the planet, not to mention the Pampers. Entire nations will be asphyxiated when the wind comes from the direction of the landfill. Some say that the destruction of the rain forest will do us in, and that despite several stern warnings made on MTV by rock stars in nonprescription glasses, the rain forests will vanish, and the world's sole source of oxygen will be a flower show in Boca Raton.
2. In order to make sure you don't hurt the earth any more than you already have, please die at the earliest possible opportunity. Have your survivors drop you off at a compost heap.
3. If we all act responsibly (see step 2) the world will be fresh and pure, and it will go back to killing us with earthquakes, floods, hurricanes, tornadoes, and volcanic eruptions.

You're probably stuck on the second point. Typical. It's just that selfish instinct that's gotten us in trouble. But if you have a pressing reason for staying around, you can at least make a few sacrifices. And I don't mean feeding Aunt Emmy to the Venus flytrap. You can:

RECYCLE. Every day, Americans use enough aluminum cans to fill the Minneapolis Metrodome thirty times over, thereby providing the Twins and the Vikings with a good excuse for performing so miserably. Of this amount, only a fraction are recycled, and of those that are recycled, 77 percent of the cans contain cigarette butts, which explains why your cola tastes funkier as time goes on.

Few people realize this, but we ran out of aluminum five years ago; most of the cans today are made from the skin of airplanes that have crashed. With most of the old aircraft being retired, however, experts expect this source to dry up soon.

And don't forget to recycle your newspapers, which can be turned into clever greeting cards and fliers urging you to recycle.

CONSERVE WATER. Long, hot showers are a sign of the profligate. Learn to take what my dad calls a "Navy shower" —which, as he tells it, consisted of three nanoseconds of water, lathering up, cleaning off with another blast of frigid water, and then jumping overboard into the Pacific Ocean.

And don't forget to put a plastic milk bottle in your toilet tank to save water on flushes. They used to advise putting a brick in the tank, but now it seems that the bricks dissolve, and the sediment clogs the pipes, gets into rivers, kills dolphins, promotes acid rain, causes large single-hulled oil tankers to veer inexplicably toward reefs, and, in general, does the things that make Jacques Cousteau look very stern and disgusted. Do we want aliens to visit earth, find a lifeless planet, and say, with sadness, "Bricks in the tank again." I think not.

These are all fine suggestions, and we would do well to heed them. Even if you think the entire ecology movement is something cooked up by a passel of Marxist cranks who want us to go back to squatting in the dust and living on lentils, you have to admit that it makes sense to reuse our materials. Look how many times Nixon has been recycled, for heaven's sake. He gets put out on the curb every five years, only to come back good as new. A word, then, for conservative Republicans: treat the earth as though it were Nixon.

The Democrats already have a lock on the ecology movement. If the conservative attitude toward nature has been "Pretty. Now hand me the chain saw," the liberals have always been tree-huggers. Worst are the radical groups, who would rather you get gangrene than some helpless mold be slaughtered to make penicillin. And no chopping that leg off—that's the gangrene germ's natural habitat.

Given a choice between the two positions, I'd have to go with the liberals on this one, even if it means casting my lot with the pro-lichen crowd. They believe global warming is coming, and we should either change our ways or coat ourselves with the Colonel's special blend of eleven herbs and spices and prepare to be fried. If they are wrong, fine. Better that than saying global warming needs more study, and ending up twenty years hence reading travel stories on "Anchorage: Rio of the Pacific Northwest."

If the environmental movement makes us determined to act responsibly and not foul this sandbox, fine. I just want to know what the earth is doing for its part of the bargain. The earth is hardly a benign place, you know. It bites. Just about everything on the planet either wants to kill you, or would if it could. I have no doubt that the snail darter, the spotted owl, and all other species we've gone twice around the block to save will someday evolve to our level—at which point they will haul out a weapon, sneer, and say, "You should have finished us off when you had the chance." And then they will eat us.

The inanimate portion of earth is no better. Earth is infantile, a spoiled brat who's had its way too long. What we call "good weather"—sunny skies, no wind, pleasant temperatures—is really the earth taking a nap. *And it looks so innocent.* Wake it up, and it howls, throws tantrums: earthquakes that swallow the helpless, storms that pelt you with ice and lash you with bitter wind. Earth at these times seems to regard us like a rash it can't keep from scratching.

So, no, I don't trust the earth. You can't reason with it. The next time a tornado snakes toward my house, I don't expect my running out and saying, "But I recycled!" to make much of an impression.

How about a deal: we'll knock off the polluting, and the earth will cease to play skittles with trailer parks. I think we can swing a good deal.

No more Pampers, Earth. And that's our final offer.

S&L to Pay

━━━━━━━━━━━━━━━━━━━━━━━━━━━━━━━━━━━

YOU KNOW BY NOW THAT THE COST OF THE S&L BAILOUT will be $2,000 for every man, woman, child, dog, insect, and single-celled organism in the land. And what do we get for our money? Nothing. Not one public hanging. Not one S&L officer in the stocks, bedecked with the hot spit of passersby. Not even the satisfaction of knowing that the guilty men have been sent to a prison filled entirely with psychopaths who have been refused bank loans.

What we get are calluses from shoveling money into the pockets of people who were too stupid to watch their money in the first place. The Silverado Banking, Savings and Loan Association of Denver, a thrift that collapsed with such vigor that buildings swayed a hundred miles away, is a perfect example of a stupid investment. Silverado is no name for a bank. It is a name for a gift shop in Arizona. Real banks have names like the First National Bank of Eternity. Thrifts have names like First Local Strip-Mall Drop Box of Tuesday.

But this mess can't be blamed on the poor souls who put their money in thrifts. It's the wretched swine who took the money *out,* often by bucket brigade. Frequently they were assisted by folks like Neil Bush, the president's son and Silverado's director. I don't think ill of the man; he looks as though he wouldn't harm a fly. Particularly when he could loan that fly several million dollars. Silverado operated, like most S&Ls, in some bizarre parallel universe where all the laws of banking were reversed. Here, I can say with some confidence, is what a typical meeting with a Silverado executive was like:

"We'd like to borrow a billion dollars."

Silverado executive starts to write the check, pauses when he gets to the "memo" portion in the lower left-hand corner. Says: "Ah, what is this for?"

"A condominium complex in the town of Slim Pretext, Arizona, population three. It's six hundred miles from any sizable urban center. We plan to construct seven hundred thousand luxury condominiums. Actually, we just plan to buy some lumber, truck it to the site, and leave it there."

Silverado executive, befuddled, wonders if he should be concerned. "Well . . . how are these condos to be built?"

"Superman will come and do it in an afternoon, and for free."

"Ah! Well, that's fine. If Superman is on your team, why, that's all the collateral we need."

This scene was repeated over and over again in thrift offices across the land. But how did the S&Ls come up with the money to loan? Simple. They sold bonds, which are extremely detailed pieces of Monopoly money. The bonds no doubt had a picture of a grim mythical figure, the words PAY TO THE BEARER, and the phrase ONE SILVERADO WHEE-HAH BUCK! written in ornate letters.

Should you or I even think about issuing play money, the federal government would burst from the linen closet and administer a painful half nelson. But these gentlemen were licensed by the government. The Feds were in charge of making sure they didn't waste the money and have nothing to show for it. We have, after all, a Congress to do that. But it turns out that the government not only turned a blind eye to the thrifts' malfeasance, it often handed the thrift industry a poker and said, "Put 'em out!"

Again, look at Silverado. Not to pick on the president's

son—venality and corruption being the ultimate nonpartisan issue, there's no doubt that people of all political stripes are in this up to their necks. Congressional records indicate that Colorado banking officials intended to declare Silverado insolvent in 1988 but received a "mysterious phone call from federal regulators in Washington" advising them to delay the action. Need we add that this was a month before the presidential election?

All together now: *Hmmmmmmmmm.*

There's more. Neil Bush, while director of Silverado, kept mum about his business ties to two gents who eventually hoovered $106 million from Silverado. One of these stellar businessmen later put several million into a business owned by Mr. Bush.

(The sound of America stroking its chin, thinking.)

It's typical; it's pitiful. It's what happens in an age of laissez-faire. But don't think I'm going socialist on you—I am a big fan of capitalism. I believe in the level playing field.

It just drives me mad when everyone on the field is dressed like Bozo the Clown. And *we* have to pay for the uniforms.

The Good Side
of a Depression

ARE WE HEADED FOR A RECESSION? ASKS EVERY NEWSMA-
gazine, every newspaper. That's like a headline reading
AFTER 12 HOURS OF RECORD DAYLIGHT, ARE WE HEADED
FOR DUSK? EXPERTS SAY NO.

Of course we're in a recession. The economy is not just
"contracting," it's rolled up in a ball in the corner, groaning
like someone who ate a bad oyster. This should come as no
surprise; instead of spending the last ten years actually making things like steel, wrenches, and cigars, we've constructed
an economy based on junk bonds and Banana Republic clothing stores. Here comes Old Man Depression, dressed in that
new safari look.

· That's right: depression. Relieved that someone else said
it first? Confess: in the back of your mind—the place where
you keep dentist appointments, embarrassing drunken inci-
dents, the seven warning signs of cancer—you fear that something truly hideous is about to happen to the economy. If
you walked into your local bank and found the tellers spread-
ing straw on the floor because the banks had decided that

bartering with live animals was safer than accepting U.S. currency, you wouldn't be surprised.

Baby boomers in particular are terrified of a depression, because they saw what it did to their parents: it made them incapable of throwing out string. But there are some good points to a general economic collapse. If the '30s are an indication, for example, we're in for some great musicals. And there's more:

THE BLESSED DISAPPEARANCE OF OVERPRICED SPECIALTY BOUTIQUES. The boom years of the '80s cursed every city with thousands of these little entrepreneurial weeds, as real businesses like newsstands or hardware stores gave way to Armand's Shoe Horn Center ("For the discriminating heel"), where a glowering, anorexic clerk stood over a glass case of hundred-dollar shoe horns, despising you. All of these people will now have to take real jobs.

Extra bonus: the possible end of "pasta" and the return of "spaghetti."

THE PUBLIC LYNCHING OF MOST OF CORPORATE AMERICA. I think most of the stockholders would like to hold their yearly meetings under a stout tree this year. Something curious happened in the boardrooms, like one of those body-switching movies: Mr. Dither's brain was replaced by Blondie's, and corporate America decided to put everything on revolving charge.

Here's how it worked. The average food corporation of the '80s would cook up some projections that showed each American consuming thirty-seven bottles of ketchup per day by 2003, which they would then take to the banks, all of which had renamed their loan departments the Rathole Management Division. The banks would then underwrite elaborately engraved pieces of Monopoly money, called bonds, which the corporation then used to buy a healthy ketchup maker and run it into the turf.

En route, they would attempt to revitalize their company with a new product, such as a cookie in the shape of an elf. This is how it looked to the rest of the world:

Germany: rich, low debt, strong industrial base
Japan: rich, low debt, strong industrial base
U.S.A.: poor, high debt, made elf-shaped cookies

The idea was that debt would allow them to perform better. Uh huh. Sure. Just like a couple on their honeymoon is better able to consummate their marriage if you hold a gun to their temples.

If there's a depression, the business of America will be returned to stingy, top-hatted plutocrats, the way it ought to be. Warning: look out for Donald Trump in a monocle, and don't be fooled.

Public Works. Given that 80 percent of our bridges can be classified as papier mâché, we need a massive program to rebuild them, like they had in the '30s. This will give American men something vital to their self-image: a job without a hairnet.

This will require money, of course, and we don't have any. We can't go to the Japanese for spare change, since they already regard us as a weaving drunk, wheedling millions out of passersby, and they figure we'll just go blow it on unnecessary shopping malls. We can't go to the Germans, who now have to support for the national equivalent of Uncle Buck. Besides, all those bonds they bought seem to have carried the phrase REDEEMABLE FOR ONE PERSIAN GULF MILITARY ACTION, and I don't think we want to go through that again.

I say we borrow the money from the Mafia. They have the cash, and their terms are rather straightforward. Besides, I think it will add a degree of fiscal restraint if congressmen know they might get a few legs broken on the way home. And if we rebuild the bridges with substandard mob concrete, we'll have to replace them ten years down the road—thus creating more jobs. That's what I call planning for the future.

In short, a depression isn't all that bad. And it won't last long: we got out of the last one with the help of a Hitler, and we already have Hussein, who is Hitler Lite—"all the territorial ambition, with only half the scary ideology"—to get us out of the next one. It'll be a short depression. Our theme song will be "Brother, Can You Spare a—Never Mind, I Just Got a Job in a Munitions Factory."

If Poets Ran
the World

EASTERN EUROPE ISN'T JUST SHORT OF FOOD AND VCRs; they have almost no politicians left. Either the politicians have been kicked out of office or, like Romania's Ceausescu, have been marched out back and given The People's Pink Slip. As a result, the nations of the Warsaw Pact, which once led the world in the production of politicians, are now facing a shortage of politicians that threatens to plunge those troubled nations into years of happiness and prosperity.

The generous American people would be happy to crate up our spares and send them over, but Eastern Europe does not need our help. They are meeting the politician shortage with the one thing Europe has in abundance: artists.

Czechoslovakia is the best example. The first leader after the revolution was Vaclav Havel, a playwright jailed by the Communists for his work. From all accounts, he is a decent man; he has that haunted, gaunt look of the jailed idealist, and the requisite cheaply made suit that denotes membership in the Eastern Bloc intellectual community. He will, no doubt, be a vast improvement on the villains and toadies who preceded him. But putting artists in control of a nation is a dangerous act. Say Havel hires nothing but artists to fill his new government. You can expect news stories like those that follow.

Feb. 13: Czechoslovakian government decrees free refills on coffee to be mandatory, regardless of how long one has been sitting at the table. In a related act, cigarette prices are cut in half.

Feb. 15: Parliament convenes at a small café.

Feb. 16: Havel calls Parliament, feigns cold, asks for an extension on the deadline of his budgetary address.

Feb. 21: Gustav Hercok, a theatrical director, is named Minister of Defense. His first act is to replace the starched collars of the officers' uniform with scratchy black turtlenecks. Hercok does away with the draft and announces that from now on, recruits will have to pass auditions.

Mar. 2: Havel, facing immense budget deficits, calls home and asks his parents for a "loan."

Mar. 4: Famed Czech actor Spachov Merchzeck is offered the post of Minister of Heavy Industry; Merchzeck immediately moves to make the lighting in the factories more flattering.

Mar. 7: The International Monetary Fund hires *New York Times* drama critic Frank Rich to evaluate Czechoslovakia's economy.

Mar. 14: Havel's budget opens to previews in small, obscure Czech town. Frank Rich calls it "contrived, derivative."

Apr. 2: Havel premieres his new work, "The Fiscal Projections for the Republic of Czechoslovakia." One critic says that "the work seemingly consists of nothing more than a recitation of facts and figures, strung together without concern for plot or characterization." Playwright Frichek Grinchek sues Havel for plagiarism, contending that Havel lifted the budgets for mass transit and rural electrification from his 1986 musical, *Kiss Me, Lenin*. Havel's friends assure him that the critics are "just jealous."

Apr. 15: Defense Minister Hercok—the former theatrical director—inadvertently orders an invasion of neighboring Austria. The incident is cleared up when Hercok explains that his troops did not understand the difference between "left" and "stage left."

Apr. 18: United Nations envoy Neil Simon flies to Prague to punch up the budget. The result—which bases its fiscal outlays on the author's recollections of the 1947 budget for Flatbush—is deemed to be unacceptable. Czechoslovakia is plunged into an economic crisis. Entire government take jobs as waiters. Rioting mimes shot dead by security police.

Apr. 21: Havel realizes that someone left the house lights up since the revolution, prohibiting citizenry from suspending disbelief. Lights are dimmed. Budget passed without incident; only a few people leave the country at intermission.

Czechoslovakia settles down to watch the fruits of their revolution, wondering where to go for pie when it is over.

The Mysteries of
Air Fresheners

━━━━━━━━━━━━━━━━━━━━━━━━━

PARDON ME IF I PASS OUT SOON. IT'S NOT FROM ILL HEALTH, or nerves; rather, I am being suffocated by an air freshener, a little plastic obelisk with a grisly dollop of scented chemicals for innards. A sweet, cloying stench hangs in the room, as though half a dozen Care Bears died in my closet. If I breathe too deeply I'll probably develop diabetes.

Why did I buy it? Because the previous owner painted shut the windows of what is now my office at home, and I cannot get them open without incurring a hernia so severe I could be reincarnated six times and still walk with a hitch. The lack of air flow means that the room gets rather close at times; compounding matters, I smoke when I write, so after an evening's work, the room smells like someone has swabbed the walls with a moist longshoreman. I needed an air freshener.

The air freshener department at the store gave me two choices: sprays or solids. Solids are for those who are not troubled by something that simultaneously decomposes *and* smells good. Sprays are for those who don't mind destroying the ozone layer and increasing the rate of skin cancer so long as their house smells like a talcum factory exploded next door.

Each comes in the same basic fragrances: Powder, Rain, Forest, and Extra Tough. Powder smells like you'd expect, that soft scent one usually associates with cleaning up incontinent toddlers. Rain—that's the scent in my room right now—does indeed smell a little like rain when you first open the container, but after a minute it's a NutraSweet monsoon. Forest gives you the delicate, evocative sensation of being mauled by an evergreen tree.

Extra Tough smells like nothing else on this earth; it's a brawny scent that wrestles any airborne odor to the ground and pummels it into submission. The label usually says "for stubborn smells," and you can almost see the smell, snarling in a corner while the family tries to poke it toward the door with a broom handle.

Naturally, I tried each scent in the store. I sprayed a shot into the aisle, stood at the perimeter of the cloud, and sniffed. After three samples, the aisle was full of stubborn smells, and I gave it a good shot of Tough Scent. A little cloud formed, sailed off toward women's clothing, and dissolved a rack of rayon blouses.

Solids were more my style, anyway; more convenient. The scents were the same, but the delivery systems, as I'm sure they call them, were different. I had discs that adhered to the wall; mushroom-shaped units, squat little cones, and something that looked like an inverted version of what the nurse asks you to go next door and fill up. The last item said "Designer Styling!" on the package; apparently it was meant for the mantelpiece.

That's the one I bought, but not for the styling. This one employed a liquid instead of a solid. This way I would not open up the container and find the skeletal remains of the freshener hanging on a stick; when the liquid ran out, the unit was no less attractive. I bought it in Rain.

There were, of course, instructions, enough to make you wonder if you should apply for an operator's license before you opened the package. The most demanding instruction dealt with the vents on the side of the unit. There were no less than five different levels of Rain I could release into my house. I set the thing on 5, put it under the desk in my writing studio, and went downstairs to make supper.

Five minutes later I got a phone call from the folks down the block; they asked if I wouldn't mind setting the freshener on 3, or 2. I apologized and headed upstairs to turn down the volume. I never made it past the first landing. A roiling miasma of Rain had occupied the upstairs of the house, a smell of such density you required deep breaths from a tube of airplane glue to clear your mind. I didn't even bother trying to get up there; I drove to the store and bought a vial of Tough Scent. I lobbed it upstairs like a grenade and hid in the basement the rest of the night.

I've since thrown away the vial of Rain. It leaked into the garbage can, and now the can smells like a combination of Life Savers candy and wet dogs. But wisps of Rain remain in my room, leading me to wonder why air fresheners smell so bad.

Good question, eh? I have a theory about that. The really good smells, you see, have already been sold. There's Money, but the Federal Reserve owns that one; New Car belongs to the auto industry. Copyrights exist on all the scents worth smelling. All that remains to the air freshener industry are the bad unlicensed smells, like Hair on Fire, and Overworked Fry Cook. What you smell in an air freshener is not the result of scientific efforts to duplicate pleasant odors, but naturally occurring scents that hover just under the threshold of offensiveness.

Rain is probably something completely different, like Possum Morning Breath. As for Tough Scent, well, what do you think they do with those rags they use to mop Mike Tyson's body between rounds? You think they just *throw them away?*

Ask Dr. Dirt

━━

WHY ARE LAWN-AND-GARDEN COLUMNS ALWAYS SO SANE, so rational? I've yet to meet anyone who wasn't driven to madness by gardening. Yet most questions to gardening columns sound like this:

Dear Mr. Greenthumb:
Enclosed is a blade of a weed that has taken over my yard. I have tried spading, chemical treatment, and resodding, but nothing seems to work. Your advice?
(signed) Uncertain About a Weed

Dear Uncertain:
This is an Andalusian Oxtongue, a member of the thistle family. It can be removed from your lawn with a compound of boric acid and bacon grease and the spittle from a three-year-old; rub it into the stem until the stem is pliable. That should do it.

This is what most people want to write:

Dear Mr. Dirt:
Look at this! It's all over my lawn! Nothing works! I poured napalm on it, set it alight, dug up the lawn, paved it over,

moved to another town, and I still can't get rid of it! What the hell can I do?

(signed) Hyperventilating

Dear Hyper:

You are doomed. This is a weed called Satan's Nosegay, and it is renowned for its ability to encircle your foundation with its roots. Eventually, if untreated, it will pick up your house and move it across the property line. (Scientists have this on time-lapse photography.) It is also the only plant known to be capable of phoning a lawyer and having you sued. The only thing you can do is consult an exorcist; most chemical lawn-care companies have one on call.

That is what people really feel, but they don't put that emotion into their letters. Likewise, they keep their personality out of the matter. The following series of letters to Dr. Dirt illustrates the breadth of lawn-care questions we receive that must go unanswered because they don't fit the profile.

Dr. Dirt:

Thank you, thank you, good evening, you're looking great! Hey! Thank you! Hey, a funny thing happened to me on the way to the garden, I gotta tell ya. Anybody here tonight have a garden? Okay. So I got these weeds, and I'm pullin' 'em up, right, and they've got some long roots. I figure maybe I've uncovered a buried clothesline, okay? I mean these roots go all the way to China. Probably have a sinkhole in Tieneman Square after I get done. Ba-boom!

(signed) Wacky

Dear Wacky:

Based on the sample you sent, I think you have a problem with Hardyharhar (Latin name, *Buddae hackettus*). This is a pesky weed, indigenous to Los Angeles and Las Vegas. As to getting rid of it, that's simple. If you want it to die, put it in front of a crowd that's completely sober.

Dr. Dirt:

As a Marxist, I find my garden a raging hotbed of inconsistent philosophies. On one hand, you have the flowers, the blooming of which is the supposed goal of the garden; on the other hand, there are the weeds, indomitable, hardy, but unable to exist with the flowers without overrunning the area.

If communism is truly applicable to every sphere of life, then should I not give the weeds the run of the garden? After all, the flowers are obviously the bourgeoisie of the plant world: frivolous, devoted to appearances, requiring maximum labor for minimum return. The weeds are clearly the proletariat, and I should applaud their ability to thrive in an unfair environment.

I feel as though I should purge the flowers, and make a political example of my garden. On the other hand, the begonias are just fabulous this year.

(signed) Prof. A. Dumont, Department of Radical Agronomy

Dear Prof:
Lenin had a lot to say about gardens. It was Lenin who said, "Comrades! En route to consolidating the gains of the revolutionary struggle to achieve the dictatorship of the proletariat, stop! Find roses! Smell them!" So don't worry. Flowers are not inconsistent with communism. Just take care that your weeds do not spill into your neighbor's garden. It is difficult to explain that the goldenrod choked his snapdragons because it was their internationalist duty.

Dear Dr. Dirt:
The last time I was at the garden store, I saw a bag of something called Weed 'n' Feed. I gather it kills the weeds and nourishes the good plants. Since then I have been unable to sleep, as I am tormented by the question: How does it know what to feed and what to kill?

(signed) Haunted

Dear Haunted:
It just does.

Dear Dr. Dirt:
I got these weird weeds that grow through asphalt. I can't get my grass to grow on soil, and here's something that grows

on asphalt. Of course it's ugly. The hardier the plant, the uglier it is. Maybe there's a lesson there.

I wouldn't worry about the ugly weeds if my flowers could at least stay alive. But all my flowers formed a suicide pact. No one has yet done any research on this, but I know the truth, I know that plants can commit suicide. Most flowers, in fact, die by suicide. Pull them up after they've died, and you'll see they've tied granny knots in their roots. Do they leave notes saying, "Now that I've bloomed, there's nothing more to live for?" No. They make us feel guilty.

I had a window box of red something-or-others—Nasteraniums, or Bachelor's Spats, or Geronigolds, I don't know, the wife picks them out. Anyway, I watered them daily, just like it said on the little plastic spear. They died. They looked like I went out there with a blow torch and gave them a good shot of fire every morning. We bought some impatiens—I remember the name of those because it sounded like a flower that would always drum its leaves nervously, thinking, "All right, all right, where's the water, where's the sun, I don't have all day." I watered them. They died.

I bought some tropical-looking numbers. The plastic spear had a picture of a dark sun, which I took to mean shade, so I planted them in the shade. They died. Only when I read the spear did I realize the little dark sun means they only thrive during a solar eclipse. The people who run the country know this. They don't tell us.

So everything died. The little plastic spears were just tombstones. I would look out the window and expect to see little clumps of flowers from the garden next door laying wreaths under the plastic spears.

So now everything is weeds. Hardy weeds. These are the boors of the plant world, the plant equivalent of the guy who comes over unannounced, puts his feet up on the table, and yells for a beer. These are the plants that grow right next to the flowers in your garden like they're trying to pick them up. Hey, baby: sprout here often?

They haven't just taken over the garden; they own the lawn. My lawn is all weeds. I console myself with the article I read in magazines many years before, about how plants feel pain. I tend to feel that a proper, domesticated lawn suffers a mow like a good dog suffers a haircut or bath. Weeds are craven

and cowardly, and fear mowing. So I mow with a sneer. I set
the blade real low. When I am done mowing, I yank them up
by hand. Reallll slowly. Then I put them in plastic bags so
they will not decompose but be entombed in landfill for a
millennium or more.

But that's over now. I sold my house. I live in an apartment.
I might be happy someday.

(signed) Hates Weeds

Dear Hates:

I've examined the sample of weeds you sent, and they are
Appalachian Oil-finders (*Clampettus jed*). They usually grow
over large reserves of unrefined petrochemicals. Pity you
moved. With all that oil wealth, you could do what most
people want to do: have someone come in every week, tear
up the lawn and gardens, and put new ones down. That is,
after all, the only way you can keep your landscape perfect.

3

PRIVATE
LIFE

I never know how to respond when people tell me they want their journals burned after they die. And, yes, it does come up often in conversation; I travel in a very self-conscious circle, where not having a policy about the disposal of one's journal is like not having an opinion on the destruction of the rain forest. In fact, it's often the people who oppose the burning of the rain forest who write the most journals, and who want them burned, thereby contributing to global warming. Go figure. But I think I lost my original point.

I never know how to respond, etc. Well, what do you say when someone wants their journals destroyed? My original reaction is that there must be entries about rubber undergarments and the Carpathian Catheter Manufacturers' Convention, and the person I am talking to is an utter deviate. Their journals are probably too damp to burn, and should be handled with tongs by men in lead suits, and placed in a mountain somewhere with a plaque full of symbols to warn future generations. How we can communicate the notion of latex underclothes to people ten thousand years hence, I have no idea.

Most people, of course, are simply blowing smoke, because (a) they have no intention of dying anyway, and (b) their journals are of interest only to a few people who did them wrong, and those individuals will be liver-spotted, sexless, and napping in an Arizona retirement community by the time the journals become available for public consumption. But to say you don't have a policy on your journals is to imply that you will never be famous, and that no one will care one way or another what you wrote.

Most people with a policy believe they will be famous, or at least are holding out for Boswell status. Boswell, as anyone out there with an English degree is probably congratulating themselves for knowing, was a guy who hung around in a coffee shop frequented by Samuel Johnson, a warty old codger who

144

wrote the first English dictionary. Boswell kept journals that are invaluable for their look at Johnson and eighteenth-century London life; they are also notable for Boswell's kinetic and vaguely pathetic sex life. Seems the young man would abstain until steam curled from his nostrils—this could take as long as a day—and then would hurl himself at the nearest prostitute, run home and write pages venting his shame. Good part: for his interesting life and proximity to greatness, Boswell has been remembered through the ages. Bad part: several centuries later, bitter graduate students in a poorly heated classroom lead healthy young people through a snickering account of his sex life.

I want mine burned, but for different reasons. I simply do not want to bore anyone. Reading my journals is like standing in front of a firehose gushing with oatmeal—plenty of volume, none of it interesting. They consist mostly of complaints: *no girlfriend,* then *bad, bad girlfriend.* In between there are brief patches of *yea, girlfriend!* but you can pick up a greeting card and get the idea. I stopped writing journals when I met my wife and got on to the business of having a life instead of treating it like background information for one of those panel-discussion shows you see on Sunday morning.

All of which is a roundabout way of saying that a section called "Private Life" is bound to be disappointing. My private concerns—love, money, hair—are mundane and unexceptional. In fact, should I unexpectedly expire after this book comes out, I've considered asking the publisher to burn all copies, just to increase whatever reputation I have achieved.

Either that, or I have lived an extraordinary life, rich with secrets, and I'm not only hiding a lot from you, I've rigged my bookshelf to go off the moment anyone attempts to pull out a journal without entering the proper security code combination.

I don't know about you, but I always felt bad for Boswell.

I Am Not Going Bald,
I Am Not Going Bald,
I Am Not Going Bald

I AM NOT GOING BALD. I SAY THAT IN THE SAME SPIRIT that a condemned man in the death cell, listening to them crank up the electric chair, says, "I am not going to die." No, it can't happen to me. The governor will ring up a few minutes before midnight and grant me a full and unconditional head of hair.

Denial, of course, is the first stage of baldness, followed by depression, quack cures, small fast cars, and obvious toupees. It ends in acceptance, which comes when you find yourself using mirrors to catalog the interesting port-wine birthmarks you never would have seen if you still had your hair.

I'm not that bad, yet. But I am at the stage where I am acutely aware that "hair" is both singular and plural; when someone says, "I like your hair today," I wonder if they have a particular strand in mind.

Going bald is a touchy thing for a man, and don't let anyone tell you otherwise. There's nothing good to be said for it, except that you get more for your money in a tanning booth. And maybe you can write 39 AND HOLDING! on the

147

back of your skull, add some silver paint, and hire your-self out as a mylar balloon. Other than that, I see no advantage.

This started early. In high school. Some genetic code went forth, inviting my hairline to meet my neck. My mother asked her hairdresser for a good remedy. This was a woman much like Madge, the brassy manicurist of the Palmolive com-mercials, only worse. ("Caustic lye? Of course, it's mild. You're soaking in it.") Not exactly a medical expert. She gave my mother a secret cure: raw egg rubbed daily into the scalp, in the morning, before the sun got too high.

When I heard this, I inquired if eye of newt and wing of bat were also required. I wanted hair, Mom, but it was not worth my immortal soul. (I still had a lot of hair when I said that.)

My mother was insistent. "It's the protein," she said. I noted that meat also had protein, but I was not about to wear a fedora stuffed with ground chuck.

Instead, I wore a hat stuffed with raw egg. Yes, I gave in; such is desperation. I spent every morning of the summer of 1975 wearing a plastic hair-dryer cap, watching game shows, raw egg running down the bridge of my nose. I could never wash the smell out. I would pass fry cooks on the street and they would, by instinct, tuck a sprig of parsley behind my ear.

It did not work, of course. But that hairdresser's advice was better than the line I got from a stylist I met a few years later. She peered at my forehead, scowled, and said that my brain was siphoning off precious nourishment that should have fed my scalp. If I could cut down the flow of blood to that greedy old brain and divert it to my follicles, I would have luxurious hair. It may sound odd today, but at the time there was evidence supporting this position, most notably the posters of Farrah Fawcett.

What she prescribed, really, was an occasional scalp mas-sage. I spent a year massaging my skull whenever I had a chance, looking like a man plagued by demons or the need to write poetry. I succeeded in crushing the few remaining hairs that were homesteading on my frontal pate.

That was a few years ago. I am not much balder today than I was then ("then" being defined as the last time I really looked in the mirror), and I don't care. I'm married, and I no longer need to regard my hairline as a job-seeker would regard a typo on his résumé. I yam what I yam, to quote another short, bald guy who brooked no ridicule. But what if I wanted to be more?

There are several options. Minoxidil, for example. This is the stuff that will grow hair on a brick, particularly a brick with a liberal health-benefits plan. Of course, you have to apply it for the rest of your life, or your new hair falls out. It is as close as men will ever come to understanding the Pill.

Minoxidil is completely safe, according to the FDA, but when you realize that it was originally a high-blood-pressure medicine intended for oral ingestion, you wonder: (*a*) Did the people who originally tested it as an oral drug end up having to wash and set their soft palate every day? and (*b*) If not, how did they discover it grows hair?

I mean, I can't imagine that the FDA routinely takes all substances up for approval and rubs them on the head of a bald man, just in case. ("Whoa! This one dissolves bone on contact!") More likely, someone spilled it on the workbench, returned the next day, and found a disembodied Mohawk sprouting from the Formica.

There are transplants, but they're painful. They use a follicle version of a backhoe to remove hair from your upper neck and plant it on your forehead, much like those old Punch-n-Gro seedling boxes.

You could get a rug. A toup. A Howard Cosell–approved vinyl helmet. But then you have to live with your wife saying, "Honey, give me your hair, I'm doing a load of synthetics."

Most suspicious, to me, are those hair-weaving or -stranding stores, the ones that run cheap boldfaced ads and are run by someone whose head looks like a Brillo pad was forcibly integrated into his genetic structure. I actually called one of these places and asked what was involved.

"Well, first," said the man on the phone, "you'd come on down and we'd analyze your hair to help us find the best treatment." And how is my hair to be analyzed? "On a scale of 1 to 10."

Ah, of course. And if I have a 1?

"If you have a 1, then you probably don't have any hair at all." That is downright oxymoronic: *We have analyzed a sample of your hair and determined that you do not have any.* If I can wrap my brain around that, I can probably construct some metaphysical puzzle that not only proves I have hair, but that God exists.

I am currently less than utterly bald, so I don't worry about this all the time. But I know there will come a day when I look in the mirror and see altogether too much skin. When that day arrives, I will do everything but glue hair-colored pieces of crinkled tissue paper to my skull. Because—and this is the point—I really do not want to be bald.

Whatever method I choose—toupee, weaving, transplants, FDA-approved goop—I know I'll never be able to go home. I couldn't bear running into my mother's hairdresser and having her believe that the goddamn eggs *worked.*

Learning to Hate
at Bible Camp

IT WAS AT BIBLE CAMP THAT I FIRST LEARNED WHAT IT felt like to wish someone dead. Probably not what the counselors had in mind.

For seven summers, I attended White Earth Lutheran Camp. The years have smeared the memories together; when I think of camp, I am perpetually ten, fat, and grinning. I'm at an age when a day of summer lasts longer than I do, and the sun hangs in the sky like a pop fly that would never come down. I have a top bunk, and life is perfect.

Except for John Larson and Charlie Brown.

John Larson was the Mean Kid. He went to my school, he went to my church, he showed up at camp. No escaping the little swine. He was the sort to yank up your underwear when the elders weren't looking; he walked like an ornery drunk, and he cussed. He was ten.

The first night of camp, he decreed that I should have the honor of finding a snipe. The other kids in the cabin, apparently bucking for merit badges in sadism, roundly agreed, and I was given a bag and a stick. I was to go out into the woods and beat the side of the bag with the stick, and snipe aplenty would hurl themselves into the bag. I nodded and headed into the woods. I had no idea what I was doing.

It was, of course, a horror-movie night—wind and leaves arguing above my head, thunder muttering on the horizon. I walked along, beating the bag, probably calling for snipe. Here, snipe. *Nice* snipe. Nothing. Just wind pushing me deeper into the woods with rough hands. I turned around; I couldn't see the lights of the cabin. The trees were holding their hands over the moon; I had no light by which I could see the path. Terror scrambled up my throat, and I fled in terror for the cabin. As I ran I thought I heard something pass me in the dark, crashing through the grass at my feet —small, terrified, darting for shelter. A snipe.

I burst into the bright light of the cabin, panting; everyone was sitting on their bunk, grinning, waiting. "Get a snipe?" said John Larson.

"No." Pantpantpant. "But I think I saw one."

Raucous laughter. At that moment, I got it. There was no snipe. That was the joke, and it was on me. But something *had* passed me in the dark, and I *knew* it was a snipe. That was the other joke, and it was on them.

Standard casual cruelty, the sort of thing kids do to each other all the time. I almost want to thank that sorry crew for sending me on that mission; the moment when I stood in the woods convinced that Satan was coming down to give my soul a mean Dutch rub is one of the most vivid memories of my life, a socket that still carries current. But I really could have done without Charlie Brown.

Mr. Brown was a counselor. Stolid, bearded. Not too jolly. One night—I don't remember which year, but John Larson was there—we were all gathered at the lake for evening service, when Mr. Brown interrupted the devotions. In a tight, grim voice, he said he had something to announce. A few kids laughed; Mr. Brown barked out a shut-up and stared over the assembly.

"A few minutes ago," he said, "a missile was accidentally launched from Russia. It is heading toward Minnesota. It will be here in about twenty minutes."

I felt mercury sluice down my backbone. Just the day

before I had been badgering the camp pastor about whether the end of the world was due anytime soon, like before my birthday. He'd said there was no indication, as far as he knew, and that I should go play tetherball. He'd lied. He knew.

"I'm afraid you will never see your families again," Charlie Brown continued. "It's time to make your peace with God."

Endless minutes of silent prayer followed, punctuated by sniffles and gasps. Mr. Brown stood there, head bowed, presiding over the mute and frozen panic of a hundred children. Finally he raised his head, said that it was not true. No missiles were coming.

"But what if they were? Would you be prepared to meet God? Is everything right in your heart?"

Not at that moment. Everyone wished Mr. Brown dead. When we were back at the cabin, John Larson said, "I would like to cut him open and watch him float belly-up." I agreed. We all agreed. The next year Mr. Brown was not among the counselors. The year after that, John Larson stopped going. I have no memories of anything that happened at camp after that.

I'd intended to write about the sunnier recollections of camp, but it turns out that this is what I remember best. Fine; no need to romanticize your childhood, pretend you were nothing but a carefree little idiot with scabby knees and a tan that stopped at my shirtsleeves. I know I was that as well, but that's never the whole story. Some memories tell you who you think you were, a picture without shadows. Others have a light so bright and vivid you see shapes lurking in the wings—shapes you couldn't name then and couldn't name now. Shapes you'll meet again, that will speak as they did when you were a boy of ten, trying to put it all together. Wind. Path. Light.

Halloween

IT TAKES NO GREAT INSIGHT TO NOTE THAT PEOPLE'S HAL-loween costumes say a good deal about what they want to be. The couple that shows up as a pair of parentheses wants the world to know they have a relationship so insular and exclusive that they view the entire world as being teamed against them, and have perhaps resorted to Amway to strike back. Then again, if they are standing in a way that forms a)(, perhaps they are advertising for new partners.

All I know is that if someone dresses up as Gilligan, you should take his word for it; if someone comes dressed as a product of thirty-two generations of Appalachian inbreeding, replete with corncob pipe and Li'l Abner clothing, you should keep him away from the couple dressed as Salt & Pepper lest he start an argument about miscegenation and God's intentions. And when someone shows up as Death—and someone always does—you should stay away. These people are trouble.

I knew Death at the last costume party I attended. He had a room upstairs. He made for a hearty Death, as though he was making Last Call out of duty but knew a great after-hours joint. Still, there is something unnerving about know-

154

ing that the gentleman dressed as the Grim Reaper is, in real life, a repossess man. You figure maybe he's been promoted and these are his new work clothes. What is death, anyway, but someone coming in the night, hot-wiring your soul, and hauling it off to the impound lot of limbo?

He laid a hand on the shoulder of everyone he passed. "You are next," he said. He'd turn to someone else and say, "Your time is soon." Everyone laughed. He was, after all, not entirely grim. More like the Three-Sheets-to-the-Wind Reaper. He took up residence around a keg of beer and granted a few more years of life to all who approached the keg. Later he took the dance floor and did the usual spasmodic twitch to "Burning Down the House" by the Talking Heads. People worried about whether Death was fit to drive, but were reassured that Death lived here. When I left the party, Death was sprawled in the corner, talking to one of the parentheses. They seemed to be hitting it off.

I had spent the night dressed as a 1920s society figure— tux and top hat, walking stick and white gloves. A tape player and a set of small, tinny speakers in my jacket played old jazz, but the party was too loud for the music to be heard. When I left the party and stepped outside I heard the music for the first time in hours, a thin thread of gaiety unraveling inside my costume. I looked up at what was left of Halloween night—a calm, half-finished moon in the sky, a few rough drafts of clouds, the trees still and untroubled by wind or gusting spirits. Nothing on the street but empty shadows, indifferent darkness. It was an adult's Halloween. October 31. Rent was due tomorrow.

I don't believe that everything was better when you were a child. Holidays are usually stacked in favor of adults. Most holidays meant tight clothing and the small table with the rest of the kids. No matter how much you enjoyed it, adults always had a corner on the Real Meaning, and they kept it to themselves in circumspect gatherings. The Adults in the Living Room, with their smoke and amber potions, owned the holidays. They doled them out to you in generous, indulgent doses, but it was their name on the owner's card, and you sensed that.

But Halloween was yours. By definition. There was no church attached, which was your first clue; the purpose was *candy,* which clinched the deal.

You knew it wasn't a holiday on the order of the big ones, for school wasn't canceled to let you enjoy it. But school recognized its importance, and made room. When art period came, it was not block prints with carved potatoes or crayon drawings, but ghosts. Orange and black appeared in the schoolroom, colors the world was assuming on its own, now given a delicious shiver of mystery. You carved pumpkins, let the seeds dry, ate them, their salty taste almost the taste of the leaves you kicked through on your way to school each morning. Somehow you sensed a natural progression to life—the anticipation of Halloween, the sober duty of Thanksgiving, the deep delights of Christmas. That was how it was last year; that was how it was always going to be.

A decision was due: your costume. A hobo? Too obvious. Someone else was always a hobo. Dracula? Good, good, but, like Frankenstein and the Wolfman, they were year-round figures, always there. You went down to the store— the Ben Franklin if you had one—to see what had come in.

There was always a seasonal row at Ben Franklin, a hall of worthy merchandise. In a few months it would be full of silver baubles and tinsel, and right after Halloween there'd be nothing but stupid turkeys in buckled shoes. But for now it was just right. Forbidden things: fake scars, fake blood, fake faces of disfigurement and horror. All those things that happened for real somewhere out there, somewhere beyond the Living Room of the adults, here for you to wear and reap your reward.

The great debate of childhood: Homemade or from a box? A costume from a box was the height of cool until you put it on. There was no feeling like toting that box home and looking at it each day, waiting, waiting. You were going to be the meanest superhero or the most beautiful princess. But after school you tried on the mask that came with the box —just for a few minutes, so as not to spoil it—and, well, to be frank, it lacked. Your breath was hard to draw, the air you took in had a plastic tint, and the edge of the mask was sharp and unfriendly.

The demands of the profession, you figure.

The days pass with the infuriating deliberateness of all things designed by adults. When Halloween comes, there is no rain to keep you inside—it never rains on Halloween.

One year I remember, I was Spider-Man—store-bought mask, costume homemade from old blue pajamas. Cousin Keith was a hobo, homemade all the way. In the photos in the scrapbook we are hoisting pumpkins in the air, grinning, the neighborhood still unplundered. With the floating circle of the flashbulb still drifting in our eyes, we set out to Trick or Treat. He has a cool plastic pumpkin. I have a bag with a cackling witch on the side.

There is, if I remember this right, a pumpkin in almost every window. Paper ghosts and cats, backs arched in warning, hang in the windows. Scary old neighbors who never wave when you pass them by don't put out pumpkins, and we pass them by. But the rest of the street is ours. Dark by choice. Every house with a jack-o'-lantern is another promise kept. *They knew it was our holiday; they've done this for us.* All that remains is to pretend to scare them.

We arrive at the doorstep with other kids from the block, judge their costumes, cast quick looks at the depth of the booty in their bags. We ring the bell. When the door opens we say the word—*TRICKATREAT*—and the adult is properly horrified. We know we don't scare them. But there is the moment when they open the door, when our voices combine, when we all know we have a moment of anonymity and power, and that makes us believe in the fierce determination of our little masks. We are rewarded, and we scamper away. We say thank you first.

No one here believes in the faces, the witches, the ghosts—that's for babies. But we all agree there is something out there. Something between Dad in the car down the block and the cold sliver of moon. There *is* something scary in the leaves in the gutter, the sharp command of the wind, but no one quite knows what. There is the sense that if you take Halloween on the terms you've made for it, it's kid stuff, and if you imagine there's something else, you don't get it. Yet.

These are not things you dwell on. There is still the mysterious territory of the houses on the other side of the block. And there is Dad in the car. Your breath is hot under your mask. Tomorrow there will be all the candy you couldn't eat tonight.

Adults have Halloween rituals of their own. They show up as what they want to be, what they can't be, what they fear, or as an exaggeration of how they think the world sees them. It is dress-up and it is harmless. Some religions celebrate Halloween and others condemn it as the Devil's work. Most of us note its arrival and departure through the displays in greeting-card store windows.

But it's one of the few times that asks us to go back and recall. It's one of the things in life so germane to childhood that no one ever measures an adult Halloween against those of years long ago. All that candy is bad for you, anyway.

There is always one Halloween in your life, however, when you realize that the house at the end of the block is dark, and you are not certain whether those headlights at the other end of the street are Dad's. For one moment the mask matters little and the bag of treats is heavy. At that moment something is planted inside you, something that will blossom years later and make you laugh at the repossession man when he enters the party, laugh, and give him a drink and try to get on his good side. That seed tastes pulpy and salty, strange, like the taste of fallen leaves you kicked through with great determination.

Autumn

AUTUMN IS A BOOK WE NEVER GET TO FINISH. MOST YEARS, winter slams the book shut just as we're starting to understand the story. This year, where I live, it was better than most: autumn lingered and let us read the book at leisure, savor each page. The story was old and familiar, something told by a distant and benevolent parent. We always fall asleep in the middle.

Last week I woke up to find winter moving in. Snow was falling, wet snow that vanished the moment it touched the pavement. Whatever accumulated on the lawn was erased as the day grew warmer; this was just a first draft, winter's opening remarks. But I looked around and saw bare trees, and wondered when *that* had happened, when the last leaves had fallen. I hadn't seen it happen. When the sun set, its colors were pale and weak; the sun of autumn had been rust and umber. I hadn't noticed the day it lost its luster. I could name the day when winter came, but had no idea when autumn had left. I never got to finish the book.

This is probably the wrong time to start complaining about winter. No one will take me seriously. If I gripe about winter before the first blizzard, I am obviously no true Minnesotan. A Real Minnesotan runs out into the first snow and sticks his face in a drift. Complain, and you are an outsider, the beggar at the party. Well, I am not a true Minnesotan. I am by birth a North Dakotan, a state whose climate makes a St. Paul winter look like a Bahamas getaway. And I'm not a true Minnesotan in another sense: I don't like to lie about how much I love snow. I regard my tenure in this season, my ability to survive winter without dying or moving, as having less to do with my character than the availability of heating fuels and the inevitability of spring.

So stone me if you will, but: winter is, on the whole, an awful thing. It numbs the spirit and clogs the driveway. It grinds the mind into a thick paste of ennui, and it gives us a false sense of ourselves as a state. We don't live here because we're tough. We live here because we have mortgages.

No, that's unfair. To ourselves and to this state. Put it this way: Which month do you prefer—February or April? How do you like your trees—bare, scrabbling at the low, gray floor of the sky, or burdened with leaves, heads bowed in the vast room of a summer's dusk? Minnesota has great beauty all-year-round, and, yes, there is a certain quiet majesty to its winters. There are plenty of photo books to prove that. But few of us live in the photo books; when we look at the forests of evergreens or the even plains of snow, we see a world that few of us inhabit but all of us feel we live in. The Minnesota we know best is the urban Minnesota we inhabit each day—the streets, the lawns and boulevards, the space between our homes and our work. In those places, winter does this state a disservice. Winter comes in with a promise of beauty; before it is finished, winter makes this city ugly.

Summer, I know, can be miserable. As someone who actually enjoys the sensation of his marrow boiling, I cannot sympathize with those who suffer in heat, but I know there are people who dread the excesses of summer. But when summers are temperate, they are sublime. When winter is mild it is still cold, often gray, a long interval in the waiting room for spring. We start out like Real Minnesotans, shouting our love for the snow and the cold. By February we want a divorce. This doesn't happen with other seasons. None of us wants a season to end if the alternative is snow.

Maybe once we did love winter. I walked down to the corner market tonight as the snow fell and received a lesson in winter's beauty. It's all because of the lights, I think. Car lights, street lamps, business signs—they usher it down to the earth, give it form and motion. At the corner was a little boy and his father, waiting for the light; the boy stuck out his tongue and tasted the snow. It was new to him—if he could remember it, it was something that happened thousands of years ago, when he was three instead of four. The world was instantly and uniformly different now—the same world, the same place, but remade by some benign force. That everything could change and still be the same was for him, I imagine, a source of delight, of reassurance.

We were all that kid once. I can still taste the brittle air of my snow fort, feel the bite of the snow in my boots. I can see the drifts that covered our living-room window the day of a great storm. I remember my mother going to the store for bread and milk, stocking up in advance of that storm. We never left the house that day; we *couldn't.*

There was no school. The world felt like Sunday.

A child's winter lasts no longer than it has to. The holidays give it a momentum that carries it briskly through January; the unsettling mysteries of Valentine's Day occupy you through February. During March you sense the world change; something is struggling to happen. The ice breaks under your feet one day, and you leap into frozen puddles on the sidewalk with vigor and glee. By April you don't remember winter at all. The warm and bright world you had almost forgotten is now almost yours again.

Every birthday we lament how fast the time has fled, and we voice suspicions that it is fleeing faster than it ever did. In a way, we're right. A friend of mine explained it this way: when you're five, a year is almost a third of your conscious memory. The older you get, the smaller that fraction becomes. When you're a child, a year is a second cousin to infinity; when you are an adult, a year fits between the covers of your appointment book. That book always looks so thin.

As much as time speeds up, winter takes its time. Winter passes like a long train. A child's winter passes swiftly because it is accepted; an adult's winter proceeds slowly because it is not.

This, after all, is when everything sinks into the ground and closes its eyes; this is when the turn of the earth smothers the green leaves, the soft wind. That is what winter is about. Winter kills: with a simple and elegant beauty or a harsh implacable anger, winter is here to kill. The year we realize that the path of seasons rolls over us without consultation, without heed for our needs or our desires, is the year we realize that the time we know now is not the time we had as children. We stop opening our mouths to winter when it falls, because we are afraid of how it might taste.

Most of us will make it, of course. Most of us will complain; a few will insist they find life and strength in the cold times, and we should probably believe them. Eventually spring will come, to everyone's relief and amazement. Looking at the world in winter, you'd think that spring was a conjurer's trick the earth had forgotten how to perform. But it always remembers; it knows. Just like it knows how the book of autumn ends. The last page of autumn is winter. Read it slowly, and without fear.

If a Motorcycle Is a Hog, This Must Be a Piglet

![wavy line divider]

MOTORCYCLES ARE A LEADING CAUSE OF HEAD INJURIES, you know. When I told my parents I was getting one, I heard a sharp *crack* on the other end of the line—the sound of my mother fainting, and hitting her head on the table. Helmets, I believe, should be mandatory for all parents whose children tell them they are buying a motorcycle.

It's not like I'm buying a real motorcycle. What I want is a scooter, a moped. Something with the horsepower of a blender. My reasons are solid, logical: scooters get around 73,000 miles per gallon; if you ever run out of gas, you just spit in the tank and it'll go another hundred miles. They're cheap to park; some models double as keychains and fit right in your pocket. No shelling out the daily fiver to the parking garage, no more smelling the *eau de bum* in the parking ramp stairwells. Best of all, scooters look cool.

Or so I think. The sight of a balding, thirty-one-year-old man sitting bolt upright on a bike that sounds like it's powered by an aggravated Pekinese dog is probably not what most people define as "cool," but that doesn't bother me. What does bug me are the reactions of my friends. They all see the same scenario: I'll be riding down some pleasant residential street when an eighteen-wheeled semi will leap

163

from behind a tree, whap me like a badminton shuttlecock and impale me on a lawn sprinkler.

Motorcycles are dangerous, I know. If I bought a big bike, I'd be belly-flopping into potholes the first day I took it out. But the bike I intend to buy has a top speed of 30 mph; any lower and it would have a sticker on the side reading FOR INDOOR USE ONLY. I will not be taking it out on the well-traveled streets; if I ever have to cross at a busy intersection, I'll take my clothes off, ride sidesaddle, and hold lighted Roman candles in my teeth to let everyone know I'm there.

But people just don't see scooters, my friends tell me. At first, I found this hard to believe. Most scooters are painted either radioactive-bubblegum-pink or severed-artery-red. Short of maneuvering alongside an open car window and putting your thumb into a driver's eye, scooter colors ensure you'll be noticed. Or so I thought. I have been driving around for days in my car, looking for scooters on the roads, and haven't seen one. I've even veered sharply toward the curb without warning, hoping to hear the crack of plastic and the startled *uhh!* of the driver, but I've turned up no evidence of scooters.

Evidently they represent the vanguard of Stealth technology. All the more reason to buy one. If times get tough, I can start holding up convenience stores and escaping Zorro-like on my invisible scooter.

The only bad part about scooters is buying them. You have to go to a place that sells Real Motorcycles and admit you want something cute that goes *putt-putt.* Last week, for example, I went to a showroom to look around. The room was filled with massive slices of chrome and steel leaning rakishly on their kick stands. A couple of young men wearing jackets that read JOBLESS INSOMNIACS MOTORCYCLE CLUB were listening to a salesman explain the virtues of a bike called the Banshee.

"And what were you looking for in a bike, gentlemen?"

"Wakin' people up, basically," said the thin one. "Drivin' around at night and, y'know, gettin' folks out of bed."

"Then the Banshee's your bike. She idles at 210 decibels.

Wind 'er up, and she'll peel shingles from houses ten blocks away. And it's got extra big rearview mirrors, so you can see the lights come on in houses you've passed."

"I don't know," said the other. " 'S pretty expensive."

"I'll throw in a map of all the hospitals and senior-citizen homes in the area."

They said they'd think about it and left. The salesman spotted me and strolled over. He looked me up and down and said, "Scooter, right?" I nodded. He sighed and lead me to a back room. There were cutouts of clowns and teddy bears on the walls.

"There's the Barbie," he said, pointing to a pink scooter. "Top speed of .05 mph. Runs on watch batteries." I said I wanted something more powerful, and he pointed to a scooter with MY FIRST HOG painted on the gas tank. "Pull this cord here, and it makes real motorcycle noises. You can pretend to give it oil with this bottle and nipple here, and half an hour later it wets oil on the garage floor. Very realistic."

"Something bigger, please."

"How about the EMLC 50? Perfect for a guy like you. Sporty, sexy, *with-it*. Not powerful enough to get you in trouble, but peppy enough to give an illusion of recaptured youth." I said I'd take it.

After I'd signed the papers, I asked him just what EMLC stood for, anyway.

"Early mid-life crisis," he said. "Every spring we sell a million of 'em."

God Has Call-Waiting

WHENEVER THE FUNDAMENTALISTS TALK ABOUT A personal relationship with God, they always manage to make Jesus sound like a golfing partner. I wish I felt that way. Whenever I pray I get the feeling that God is screening His calls.

As it stands now, the whole human race ought to sue God for negligence. Look at it this way: if I father a child and head for the hills before the infant is toweled off, the mother has every legal right to haul me before a court of law and demand I pony up whatever it takes to keep Junior happy. Yet God creates an entire universe, spends the Old Testament behaving in a way that should have earned Him a restraining order, then spends the last couple of millennia incommunicado. Thanks, Dad. If He had any sense at all, He would come down here and make a personal appearance once in a while, press the flesh in a few malls, do some talk shows. Take some calls.

Before you think that the hot breath of Satan roars from my every word, I should note that I certainly believe in God. But not as He is commonly perceived. Religion did its usual thorough job of warping my relationship with the divine. I grew up in a Lutheran church—or so it seemed; we actually only went on Sundays—and modern Lutheranism is a warm croissant of a religion when compared to the tooth-cracking zwieback of some other Reformation denominations. But our preacher dined on the hardtack of the Old Testament, where God behaves as though his corns are killing him. As a tot I was given the usual terrifying mixed message: (*a*) God is love; and (*b*) If you don't believe how much He loves you, you will stand in the corner for eternity. Just like being bad at school, except that your tongue will be pulled out, hot pokers will plunge into your eyes, your very flesh will boil and melt, and your butt will have an itch you will not be allowed to scratch.

That does not encourage a love of God; if anything, the child decides to stay as far away from this God fellow as possible, for He clearly has a screw loose. The God of our church did not listen to reason. "My God," I was told, "is a jealous God." Even in high school I had no idea what this meant. I had a vision of God walking into the local ice cream parlor and catching me sharing a malt with Moloch or Belial or Beelzebub, two straws, one glass, coy glances, the works. One look, and God stomps home, tears up my picture, throws himself on the bed sobbing, and vows to give all my friends eternal life.

These and other heartening tales were delivered by a pastor notable for the level of apoplexy he could sustain during a sermon without incurring a cerebral explosion. Veins like the Alaska pipeline stood on his head when he preached. Everyone left the church with windburn on their hearts, their soul smarting from getting snapped by the wet towel of righteousness. He was replaced by a bearded minister who looked like Richard Chamberlain and delivered earnest disquisitions on the evils of the Vietnam War. He had a clear vision of Hell, and Bob Hope made regular appearances there. So relaxed was this man that when he passed the communion chalice around, you half expected a line of rock salt around the rim, a slice of lime, and a parasol. He was replaced by a kindly and sexless dumpling whose sermons were thin soup, but there was no danger of him getting political or setting wives' hearts aflutter.

My faith remains undeterred. I believe in Someone Out There—call Him God, since other names, like Festus or Darrin, do not seem to fit—but am not entirely certain He is all that mindful of what goes on down here. Example: Recently a tornado destroyed a town in Texas and dropped a church roof on a batch of worshippers. One of the few things left standing were two plaster statues, one of Jesus, the other of Joseph. The townspeople, according to the news, "looked at the statues' survival as a sign of God's love."

Hold the phone. This sounds like the he-beats-me-because-he-loves-me line of thought. If the Lord in his infinite wisdom drops a concrete roof on the true believers but spares two hunks of modeling compound, it is time to question the Big Fella's priorities. If I have to be made up of plaster to command attention in this universe, something is amiss.

Which is why God should show up again. Explain that He's not in charge of the weather, or the outcome of baseball games, or marriages. That illness is not punishment but is actually heaven's version of the Daily Lotto, with the winners listed in the obituary columns.

He should do talk radio. We may, of course, not like what He has to say. If he begins the pleasantries with, "Call me Allah," for instance, dump your cosmetics and liquor stocks. Or if he says that hell not only exists, it is full, and new arrivals get to work on the new wing. Yes, hell is a union shop; why not? We've got eternity to get things done! Or maybe he'll say that premarital sex is indeed a sin, a very bad one—don't ask me why, that's just the way I am, old-fashioned, and were there any more questions about hell?

Plenty, boss. Fact is, there is information we cannot get on our own no matter how much we pore over the sacred texts. What if, for example, God said something to one of his mortal and hence fallible scribes, and it slipped the scribe's mind? The scribe has a nagging feeling he has forgotten something but does not know what it is. It comes to him on his deathbed. "The appendix," he pants, eyes rolling, brow shining with sweat. "I forgot to mention the appendix. It is the seat of the soul. Remove it, and your are damned to eternal limbo."

The doctor chalks it up to the delirium of a dying man. When the scribe dies, the doctor packs his tools and walks home, looks up in wonder at the stars. Dozens, hundreds, millions of blinking stars. In two thousand years they would remind someone of the light on the answering machine that tells you someone has called and is awaiting Your reply.

White Knuckles

I WAS WATCHING A TELEVISION PROGRAM ON PANIC AT-
tacks and phobias the other night and was amazed at the
diversity of terrors some people suffer. There was a segment
on people who are afraid to fly, one on people terrified of
elevators, another on those who can't leave the house, and
yet another on claustrophobics.

What a bunch of wimps. I'm afraid to fly, hate elevators,
used to be afraid to leave the house, and am claustrophobic,
all at once. They could have done the show on me and saved
a lot of money. I did enjoy hearing this line: "For sufferers
of panic disorders, claustrophobia—the fear of enclosed
spaces—frequently leads to agoraphobia, which is a fear of
open spaces." Got that? Fear of tiny spaces eventually in-
cludes fear of big spaces. *That pretty much covers it.*

But this was no news to me. I've had panic attacks. I had
a particularly bad one that I refer to as "the '80s." I also
have claustrophobia and agoraphobia, but let me note,
through gritted teeth, that I . . . have . . . them . . . under
. . . control. By all rights I should take my seat in the ca-
pacious confessional booth of the talk show, where Geraldo
could point to me and say, "James here never left the house
for two years, and still managed never to do the dishes."

Let's explain a few terms here before we proceed. Remember, I am not a trained professional, merely someone with years of firsthand experience, so don't take any of this as medically sound when you can have your company insurance pay for someone to tell you this.

PANIC ATTACK. Most people think a panic attack means you're Really Nervous. No. Excessive nervousness is to a panic attack what a pleasurable cleansing of your ear canal with a Q-tip is to sex after ten years in prison. A true panic attack is like something out of a horror movie: the world starts to veer around like a carnival ride, and the entire world looks as unreal as those plastic meals in Oriental restaurant display cases. You hyperventilate; your heart begins to bang away like a machine gun, your palms gush, and your extremities feel like canned hams subjected to a high-voltage electric current. As the attack progresses, you're certain you're going to die, or, far worse, throw up.

CLAUSTROPHOBIA. Most people, I think, are mildly claustrophobic. Something about nine months in the womb, I think. You'd have a hard time getting most people down in a coal mine, for example. But serious, professional claustrophobes regard any space smaller than the Astrodome as a coffin in an elevator going down a mine shaft. They fear anyplace that does not have an exit available at all times. They wish life were like a C-section: if they get in trouble, someone will take them out.

Why the need for an exit? Because you might have A Panic Attack, AND HAVE TO LEAVE BEFORE YOU EXPLODE AND RUIN EVERYONE'S SUIT. I had a perfect example of this the day I covered my first State Department briefing. I was sitting far away from the Door. Between me and the Door were a dozen network TV cameras, several burly Secret Servicemen, the Secretary of State, and fifty journalists. I realized that if I should, say, have a sudden unreasonable need to stand up, shout GODDAMN, MY HANDS ARE COMPLETELY NUMB and run screaming from the room, I would be filmed doing so by all the major networks; I'd have to bolt in front of the Secretary of State, and then be hurled to the ground by security, who would put me in a holding cell and brick up the door.

This is one way to make the evening news, but it does little for one's credibility in the media community. I did nothing, of course; I sat there and had one of those Whoa, Nellie colloquies with my heart rate, looking up at the ceiling, waiting for the forceps to come down and take me out. Beautiful ceiling. Shame to ruin it. Don't think I wouldn't have.

Mix one part Panic Attack and a soupçon of Claustrophobia, shake until demoralized, and you have:

AGORAPHOBIA. The grandpappy of phobias. With this, you don't leave home without a pack of yammering fears leaping around your heels. In fact, you generally don't leave home. Full-strength agoraphobiacs can't go out to check for mail without swooning; moderate agoraphobiacs travel far, but only when tied to a rope that's affixed to their sofa; mild cases can go anywhere, but they are in a constant state of white-knuckledness. Or they are drunk.

You might be wondering if you're phobic. Here's a small test.

1. You're in an elevator, and it gets stuck between floors. Do you:
A) Wait for help to arrive.
B) Wet your pants.
C) Wet someone else's pants.
D) Claw frantically at the door until it opens, crawl halfway out, and be dissected as the elevator car drops down, knowing in your last moment of life that at least you got out.

2. You're on a bus, and it gets stuck in traffic. Do you:
A) Sigh and open your book.
B) Sigh and open your veins.
C) Disguise your frantic shallow breaths by playing songs with a comb-and-tissue kazoo, stopping frequently to shout, "Everybody now, altogether!"
D) Claw frantically at the door until it opens, hurl yourself

into the traffic, and as you are struck by a car, know that in your last moments of life, at least you weren't in an elevator stuck between floors.

3. You're on an airplane.
A) So?
B) Yes I am, and I am very drunk.
C) I'm on an airplane? A thin metal tube way up in the air? Stop. Stop. You're kidding, aren't you? I'm not really on an airplane, am I? Oh God Oh God ohgodohgod.
D) Frantically, I claw at the door until it opens, and as the entire contents of the airplane are spewed out in a massive decompression, I am struck by a flying object and am killed; as I die I seem to be rushing through a narrow tunnel. It's one damn narrow tunnel. *Screw the light at the end of it. I'm out of here.*

4. You're driving along and realize that your road turns into a five-mile bridge with no shoulders, high above the water. Do you:
A) Put some Wagner on the tape player and adjust your breast plate.
B) Stop the car, get in the back seat, put blankets over your head, and wait for tectonic action to bring the shores of the river together.
C) Stammer, stare wildly around, run your hand through your hair until baldness results, and floor it.
D) Elevators, buses, planes, now a bridge? What kind of a sadist are you? I'd come over and punch you out, if I ever left my house again, which I won't.

It all began for me when I was twenty-five, exactly when most males start to get their first panic attack. Note I said "males," not "men." Whenever I read an article that says, "Most men have their first panic attack at twenty-five," it sounds like some milestone, some ritual of masculinity. *I'm proud of you, son,* says Dad, patting the back of his quivering, hyperventilating son.

I was sitting in a movie theater when my heart suddenly accelerated to a gallop, for no particular reason. I got up and sat in the bathroom of the theater, expecting my heart to burst out and fall flapping on the tiles like a fish on the dock. It did not. Eventually I calmed down, took my seat, only to have it happen again.

Once home I phoned a local hospital, asked for the Pointlessly Accelerated Heart division, and got a calm, vanilla-voiced nurse. She said I had probably had too much coffee. What was the movie? she asked. I said it was *Vertigo*, by Hitchcock.

"Hitchcock? Well, there you have it."

I tried to explain that *Vertigo* was not a frightening movie, more a detailed psychological study of repression, and besides, nothing was happening when I had my attack. She told me to relax, and that was it.

I turned to my girlfriend, who was twenty years old, a vigorous and vim-laden little minx about to leave for a summer in New York and who had the day before said she would be taking her birth control apparatus with her; to her I said, Now what am I nervous about?

She said she didn't know.

The next time it happened was a few weeks later, during a job interview. This time my heart not only did the zero-to-sixty in 5.5 seconds, it was accompanied by a sensation of . . . *vertigo*. Maybe the nurse had something. A month after that I was on a highway in the middle of Wisconsin, coming back from a weekend in which I found out that the aforementioned young woman had indeed been thinking ahead. I was driving alone, disconsolate, a detailed psychological study of repression, when I realized I was in single-lane traffic, with a vast National Guard convoy fore and aft, and no shoulder. I had a brain-fusing rush of synaptic gibberish —all sorts of panic signals doing a drunken cossack dance around my brain. I went numb head to toe, became unable to breathe, and did what any rational man would do: I drove into the ditch.

I stumbled out of my car, numb as a snowman, and tried to get sensation back into my limbs by *doing jumping jacks,* hoping to whip the blood into my hands. The convoy passed by, with each truck full of incredulous guardsmen watching me leap about in the ditch.

That's how it began. From being someone who used to laugh at heavy traffic—I once drove through midtown Manhattan on my way to New Jersey because I had some time to kill—I became someone who felt dry panic scrabbling at my throat if the highway was less than five lanes wide and had other cars in it. Classic progression: from panic attack to fear of a panic attack, leading to claustrophobia, leading to sitting at home for several months in a bathrobe watching cartoons. Yes, I was under medication, and I occasionally ventured out to the liquor store to fill the prescription.

Pathetic, eh? I'm much better now, thank you, having gone from being unable to cross the street with palpitations to confidently crossing the country and setting up my life anew on the East Coast, which is a sort of corporealized panic attack, a Club Dread for agoraphobiacs in which *even normal people* are afraid to leave home. I bring all this up because I think the image of me doing jumping jacks in the ditch while a military convoy passes by is an image for our times, and I want to claim it before one of those guardsmen writes a novel and swipes it.

Plus, I am doing my good deed. To my fellows in the Order of the Sweaty Palms: this can be mastered, if you just force yourself to do what scares you. Walk around with a pistol to your head for a few months. *Get on the elevator or I'll shoot!* It worked for me. I drive on highways again, take elevators, and range far from home without feeling as though my head is full of chattering wind-up teeth. I have reached my highest goal in life, which is Dry Palms.

More importantly, I'm telling you—the Normal Person— what panic disorders are. I know it's hard to understand, so let's just put it this way: when FDR said, "We have nothing to fear but fear itself," *he was really on to something*. If that doesn't make sense, then think of it this way. People with panic disorders never have to get on the bus. They get plenty of exercise from taking 300 flights of stairs every day instead of suffering the convenience of elevators. They will never die in an airplane crash. They don't have to fight traffic. Lucky folk.

If they weren't so miserable, they'd be the happiest people on earth.

4

"JOURNALISM"

I never feel comfortable being called a "journalist." That is a fine and noble calling, and requires actual work. It also requires a certain type of individual, or at least it used to. Pick up any autobiography written by an old journalist, and you will find passages like these:

I first came to the *Journal* back in 1943. It was a different place then, tougher, better. No fancy offices for us—no, we wrote on old manual typewriters by the light of our cigars. And we never greased the carriage—it took something out of your writing. You'd lubricate the thing with spit. Manly spit, the kind you get when you smoke cigars.

We wore hats then, big ones that said PRESS. No one ever knew what would happen if you did; part of the mystery of the craft, I figure.

We didn't have luxuries like phones, no sir. We conducted our interviews the old-fashioned way: we found a source, steered him into an alley, and beat the quotes out of him. They respected us for that. A man feels better telling the truth when he's wiping blood from his mouth. Nowadays, kids just call people up and ask 'em questions. Don't even so much as kick them in the ankles. And then they print what they say. No wonder no one believes what they read anymore.

We were, it goes without saying, all fabulous drunks. Hell, you weren't a newspaperman if you didn't fall down an elevator shaft at least once a month. That's why kids today have it easy—they're all sober. They don't have to grapple with big difficult words while drunk. The craft is gone. Why, I remember Jack Parker, best rewrite man we had—he drank so much he saw double, and tried to hit all the typewriter keys he saw. "Hitler" would come out "HHiittllleerr." Cross out every other letter, though, and you had some fine writing. His stories on

178

VV-EE Day alone should have won him a Pulitzer. He had a stroke once, trying to look up "Mississippi" in the dictionary.

The writing was different then. Harder, leaner. We didn't use vowels, for example. As old Ben Eisenblat, the city-desk editor used to say, "If they want vowels, let 'em listen to radio." We never knew what he meant by that. But Ben was like that: drunk, incoherent, a newspaperman's newspaperman. He was also a softy—every Christmas he'd print a whole page of vowels, so people could put them where they wanted. Gruff but lovable, Ben, and a great city-desk editor. No one knew his hometown better, no one knew where the juice was, what the dirt was, where the bodies were buried. Ben had spent his whole life getting to the heart and soul of his hometown. Which, regrettably, was Portland, Maine. We never had the heart to tell him he was in St. Paul. We'd put whaling news on the front page just to humor him.

I guess you could say we were family back then, with everyone beating up everyone else. Your editor would come back from lunch drunk and beat you; you'd get mad and beat the copy boy. The copy boy would go find some kid hawking the paper on a corner and beat him. Sometimes the whole news staff would go down to composing and beat the printers. Good times.

But times are different now, and the fact that I work for newspapers is proof. I am in the difficult position of being a fiction writer on a newspaper, hired for my ability to lie in a purportedly entertaining fashion. The good part is that I rarely have to act nice to people I am interviewing and fully intend to savage later on. The bad part is that I cannot claim that "the story isn't there" or "no one is returning my call" when I make up the story and I am the only source. Also, my editors suspect that I make up my quotes. I don't blame them.

But everyone I've worked for has made me go out and actually report stories, knowing full well I regard "facts" as the last refuge of a writer who can't make up something more interesting. They seem to regard real reporting as occupational castor oil to be hosed down my throat at every opportunity.

I am always reluctant to do it, and furious when something good results. The notion that writing about the real world can be more interesting than pulling rabbits out of his imagination is terribly humiliating to a fiction writer. Someone might confuse him with a journalist, and he would have to confess that he hadn't really earned that name at all.

The State Fair, Observed

━━━━━━━━━━━━━━━━━━━━━━━━━━━━

These vignettes are about the Minnesota State Fair, but it could be any fair in the country. They're all the same—stinking animals, bad food, raggedy carneys with more tattoos than teeth, tired sticky people moving around like drugged lab rats, pushing strollers with squalling children. I love it. I go every year, every day.

I am not sure why I like the fair—perhaps because I first visited it as a vacationing seven-year-old, on my first trip to St. Paul. Returning, two decades later, probably woke up some snoring portion of memory, which was startled into producing those Happy Child chemicals responsible for good warm memories. That has worn off, after six years of covering the fair for newspapers. But I still like how this huge town springs up overnight, the fact that it never varies from year to year, its noisy and unlettered way of bringing summer to an end.

Marching off to the fair every day to look for something to write about managed to leach away the pleasure of the event, and toward the end of my life in Minnesota I started to view the fair as Boot Camp, As Seen By Fellini. That may explain the tone of what follows.

1

The Basic Fair

It is possible to write about the fair without going there—indeed, I could do each of my upcoming dispatches without leaving my house and you'd never know. After you've been to a few years' worth of fair, you realize that the only thing that changes from year to year is the hay in the animal barns.

Yet every year the newspapers and television stations wade into the plodding crowds and try to wrest an unusual story from the event. This is what they are hoping will happen:

DATELINE: FAIR. Gunfire erupted today, high above the heads of the revelers, as rival factions battled it out on the gondola cars that traverse the fair. Water-purifier salesmen, who have occupied Machinery Hill since the fair opened, showered the beer garden with artillery shells, while heavy skirmishes broke out along the Grease Line that separates the civilian-held Grandstand from the largely Carney-controlled Midway. Hand-to-hand fighting with square yard-sticks was reported through the fairgrounds, and observers say it is the worst fighting in the 126 years of the war-torn fair.

As always, people struggle to survive. Marty Svenson, who ekes out a living by letting tanks park on his lawn, says, "As always, people are struggling to survive." But the steady stream of refugees struggling down Snelling attest to the sad fate of this once pastoral land.

That's the kind of story that does wonders for one's career. What is actually available always sounds like this:

DATELINE: A BARN. Little Billy Goodman has come a hundred miles to enter his pig Curly in the 4-H contest.

"I picked this one out special," he says. "It was kinda sickly, but me and my dad stayed up all night for three months straight nursing it back to health. Between our love and attention and about fifty gallons of growth hormones, Curly got real healthy and big."

Pride like that breeds great hopes, and Billy says he wants Curly to win. But if not, he won't be disappointed.

"It's been real special, watching Curly grow. And after I sell him to the meatpacker, I can buy some Nintendo."

Don't get me wrong. I think a world of boy-and-his-pig stories is better than man-and-his-tank tales. Freedom from random shelling is, after all, one of the things that makes the fair pleasant. It's just that there is ABSOLUTELY NOTHING NEW about the fair. The entire history of the fair can be boiled down to this:

1863: Fair starts.
1893: Electricity added.

In fact, for a single fair to stand out, it had to be canceled. Like 1945, when the fair was canceled due to war. Maybe the metal was needed for the war effort. If anyone has any pictures of battle-hardened GIs riding Tilt-o-Whirl cars across Europe, I'd like to see them. We could get one of those guys to stand in front of a car and reminisce. Great photo, good story:

DATELINE: MIDWAY. George Belkinisky remembers the time when it didn't take four tickets to get on this ride.

"We were known as the Fighting Clowns, 'cause of this decal here on the back," says Belkinisky, affectionately stroking the car on the Tilt-o-Whirl ride. "These cars were designed for rough terrain, for going up and down and around. We drove 'em from Normandy to Berlin. That's hilly terrain, and sometimes on a hill you'd get the car spinnin' around real fast. 'Course, we all had about sixty pounds of gear on, and the centrifugal force was murder. Lost a lot of good men that way."

But I'm just dreaming. In the absence of anything new, let me haul out the last, desperate measure of fair writers:

statistics. You see them every year: Five billion people will attend the fair. The animal barns will release approximately 3.4 million cubic feet of methane gas, enough to drive a fleet of 100 cars 300 miles away, where, presumably, the smell is not so bad. Over 3,323 teenaged girls who have not yet learned to say when while applying mascara will field approximately 2,345 rude remarks from the 5,320 teenage boys whose tank tops do not fully cover the midriff.

Who cares? When you hear that sixty pounds of butter will be used each day to carve the visages of the dairy princesses, do you throw down your paper, smite yourself in the forehead and race off to the fair? *Sixty pounds! I'd never have gone if they used just forty, or even fifty pounds a day, but sixty! That I got to see!*

No. You come to the fair because it's the same place you visited last year. Nothing New is the main attraction. That's what I love about it. Watch this space: absolutely nothing unexpected will follow in the next few days. As a journalist, I should be appalled at myself. As a fairgoer, I could not be more delighted.

Make that 23 percent more delighted than last year.

2

Walk, Eat. Walk, Eat.

I've invented the perfect fair food: Deep-Fried Antacid on a Stick. It combines those two crucial attributes of state-fair edibles: it has been simmered in molten beef tallow, and it is impaled on a pole. Our slogan will be "Nausea: We Giveth and We Taketh Away." Franchises now available.

It wouldn't surprise me to see such an item. I practically expected to see Deep-Fried Sushi this time out. Fair food, after all, is the American palate at its basest; everything here could truthfully advertise: "Preferred by nine out of ten Elvis impersonators." If it can be fried, it will be; if it can be stuck on a stick, it will be. Deep-Fried Stick on a Stick might be the apotheosis of this trend. Until then, we will have to content ourselves with the old familiar favorites, all listed below.

The all-time fair favorite has to be the corn dog, and no one sells it with as much as gusto as happy licensees of the Pronto Pup brand. BANQUET ON A STICK! the sign proclaims, and one's immediate reaction is, "Thanks, but wouldn't a chair be more comfortable?" There's tradition in this item, as borne out by the legend on the sign SINCE 1947. I assume that refers to the history of the Pronto Pup, but who knows? I could put SINCE 1215 on my Deep-Fried Antacid shop and be referring to the English legal tradition, which began that year with the signing of the Magna Carta. If no one asks, no one asks.

Then again, someone must have asked the people at the About-a-Foot-Long Hot Dog stands, and that someone must have been a purse-lipped, bony-faced killjoy from the Federal Truth in Wiener Dimensions Department. Everyone else boldly proclaims their dogs to be a foot in length, but all throughout the fair you find these white booths selling the About-a-Foot-Long hot dog. I have thought a great deal on the matter—About a Minute—and, discounting the compliance-with-federal-authorities matter, I have two theories. Number one: the wieners are manufactured to European standards, and are hence measured in metric. They are, in fact, 0.3047 meter long, slightly shy of the 0.3048 m needed to make a foot. Knowing that most Americans view the metric system as an agent of international Bolshevism, they wisely changed the signs. Two: they are appealing to the sense of naked, slavering greed in all of us. Sure, an About-a-Foot-Long dog could be less than a foot. *But it could be more.* In which case, you get more hot dog for your money. And if it's less? You live longer. You can't lose.

There are more modest examples of salesmanship. One

stand has a big sign with the dispirited announcement that they sell SLUSH. Presumably MUD and SLEET are also on the menu. For sheer hyperbole, however, you cannot beat Ron's Hand-Dipped Caramel Corn—imagine the work Ron goes through, laboring through the night, picking up each morsel with a tweezers, lovingly dipping it into the Caramel.

Most places, to be honest, live and die by the adjective. COLD drinks. FRESH French fries. Or CREAMY delites, perhaps the most abstract food available. After a while you expect the smoke shop to feature CARCINOGENIC cigarettes. GUT-EXPANDING beer. CIRCULAR rigatoni.

Most of these items are meant to be eaten standing up. That's the tradition of eating at the fair. Eating while you stand and walk permits you to eat more than you normally would; as we all know, nothing you eat while you walk really counts. People who would say no to one hot dog at the dinner table will, for some reason, wolf down eight while strolling around. The idea seems to be that you can work off calories by simply passing food booths, and that when you finally stop at one, you are not doing half the damage you could have done at any of the others.

So it's a wonder that there are any sit-down places at all. They exist, all right, and they are run by churches, and that lends an air of moral purity to eating there. It's usually good, stiff, starchy food, hearty fare for humble souls. I end every fair day at a Lutheran diner—partly for that hearty Lutheran java, but mostly to sit down and watch people walk by and eat. After a while, I noticed that every other person was carrying a square wooden yardstick. In all my years of fair-going I have never been given a yardstick, but I always see people carrying them. It suddenly struck me what they were for.

Fair food is bad for you, and very good to eat, right? It can be thus defined as food you wouldn't touch with a three-foot stick. They know that. *And they give you the three-foot stick.* If someone can come up with the GIANT Hot Dog on a Yardstick, they will have the fair market cornered cold.

3

The Midway of Death

"You can still get out!" the bystander shouted to the young woman. "There's still time!" She was strapped into the front seat of the Kamikaze, looking as happy as an atheist on a bus bound for Lourdes, and she shot the bystander a pleading look. *If you're going to be a white knight, buster, get off your horse.* Sitting next to her was a grinning side of beef who evidently thought this ride was almost as good as twisting the ears on the family dog and hearing him howl. His girl-friend's terror just added to the fun.

Behind them were rows of people in various states of ap-prehension. Those below the age of ten, full of blind, happy faith in all things crafted by adults, couldn't wait to go; others had the look of worn-out debauchees going through the numb ritual of pleasure. The rest had nervous grins of fear and anticipation. The carny, a gaunt, sunburned man with eyes so flat they appeared to have been tattooed on his face, stood at the gate, crooked a finger, and beckoned the rest of us to join him.

You'll find the same assortment of faces and emotions at any ride, but the Kamikaze brought it out in sharper relief, if only by the spine-draining terror of the ride. You ride a scythe in progressively larger arcs until you make a complete revolution. Simple enough. But it is fast, ruthless, and im-placable, and instead of being bounced around until you don't know which end is up, you are constantly aware of Up, and your relation to it. Hence the terror.

The woman in the first car closed her eyes and crossed her arms in front of her, and probably prayed hard enough to fuse God's beeper. When she got off, she walked five feet in front of her boyfriend—who, by then, was grinning even wider.

The Midway is the place of little terrors, a messy, howling

counterpart to the innocent exhibition barns and industrious food booths. It crouches next to the fair like a barely domesticated animal; you know you can pet it, but you never know if you'll touch the spot that makes it snap back.

Everything has an edge. The carneys, leaning from the booths like gargoyles who failed the audition, sound vaguely menacing—I mean, there's a reason these guys aren't standing in department stores offering to spritz you with cologne. Their games are all based on the come-hither of sanctioned violence. Smash this plate. Pulverize a beer bottle. Pound the mole in the hole. Pierce the balloon with the point of the dart.

The games give way to the rides—and all of a sudden the dark swirl of the carneys' voices is replaced by the smear of neon in the sky, the high wail of happy panic. Not all the rides look scary. The ride called Flying Bobs sounds like nothing more than a squad of airborne accountants—but some of them make you dizzy just to contemplate riding on them. You step up anyway and hand over your tickets.

I said *you*. Not me. I'm sure they're all perfectly safe, but I want five guys in white lab coats with clipboards and German accents tuning up each ride before I get on. The guys who run these things look like moonlighters from the River Styx Boatmen's Local.

Although—I remember the last time I took a ride on the Octopus. I was shamed into going by a girlfriend whose approach to life was a balance-bar routine on the third rail of the subway. I closed my eyes and prayed to God and sweated and swore, gripped the bar, and held on, gorge clambering up my throat. *And then the ride started.* When it was over we were left hanging in the air, waiting for the rest of the people to be let out of their cages. I could see the whole fair from up there—the double ferris wheel ploughing the night, the cable cars drifting home, the whole impromptu city of the fair set out for my perusal. When I was brought back to earth, the Midway was a different place. It still growled, and it still needed a bath. But it had a leash.

That's the point where you *start* to appreciate the Midway.

It's not, of course, about putting a leash on the beast. It's letting yourself forget the leash is in your hand.

4

Rain? No Way, Dude.

I've been a male for, oh, most of my life now, but I'm still amazed at the way some guys express their manliness. Take the three fellows standing across from the entrance to the fair, waiting for the light to change. It was raining. It had been raining for an hour. Everyone else on the corner was hunched beneath an umbrella or wearing a plastic poncho; these guys were not only without raingear, they wore tank tops. They looked impassive: *I can take a little rain. Chicks dig a guy who can take a little rain.*

That is machismo. But the one in the METALLICA: KILL 'EM ALL T-shirt was pushing a baby carriage. The carriage was open to the pouring sky, and the man pushing it realized that letting your baby float out of a carriage and sail down the street is probably not included in the definition of good parenting. He bought a newspaper from a nearby vendor and put the paper over the carriage.

The front cover that day showed a close-up photo of a man tearing into a cob of corn, teeth bared. That's what the kid looked at for the next few hours. Probably never touched corn the rest of his life.

The Men Without Raingear were not the exception. Some people refuse to believe it ever rains on the State Fair; they think normal physical laws and conditions do not apply within the gates of the fairgrounds. Wednesday was a perfect example of their beliefs: the clouds looked like a shipment of dishwater, but only a quarter of the fairgoers brought raingear. When the rain finally came, most people ran scowling and cursing for shelter, then stood looking up at the sky with sullen expressions of betrayal.

Not that the people in ponchos fared any better. For starters, the ponchos looked ridiculous, like the ceremonial robes of a sect of unusually iridescent Druids. Second, they made everyone look like a walking nose cone. Third, anyone in shorts looked as though they were walking around naked, clad only in a sheet of plastic. It makes you wonder how many people pray for a rainy day so they can walk around the fair stark naked.

As foresighted as the Poncho People may have been, there is still the matter of why anyone would want to walk around the fair in the rain, clad in a flapping piece of plastic, shielding their corn dog from the elements. The fair goes into instantaneous hibernation when it rains. The barkers sit glumly on their stools, shivering; the rides are motionless, as though reprimanded; the food booths draw plastic curtains across their open windows. Nothing tastes as good when it's raining, anyway. Rain pools on the grass, beads on the benches, drips from trees. If this were a family picnic, everyone would have packed up and left by now.

But no one leaves because of the rain, and people keep coming. Most have umbrellas. A few men arrive in trash bags and caps, grinning at how foolish they look. Some women push baby carriages wrapped in plastic, the baby's breath steaming up the plastic and making it look as though the women have brought their favorite plants in a portable hothouse. These people have come for the fair, and they will take no argument.

The fair obliges, as best it can. Over at the band shell by Machinery Hill, a band is tuning up for an afternoon concert. It is a nightmare of a gig—there's no one in the audience but seven teenage girls, all of whom are perched on the rim of the stage, giving molten looks of admiration to the musicians. Off to the left of the stage is a gigantic balloon of a dog used to promote beer; he's face down in the mud, his tongue lolling out.

None of this matters to the seven girls. The inclement

weather gives them an excuse to hug the stage, sit like aco-
lytes by the speakers. They greet every sound the band makes
with a whoop of appreciation. This is the only audience in
the world that applauds after a band has finished tuning.

The guitarist steps up to the microphone.

"It's *cold* up here," he says.

"WHOOOO!" the girls reply.

"How you all doin'?" he shouts. "You cold?"

"WHOOOOO!"

The band members look at one another, shrug, and start
to play. A few of the Poncho People drift to the periphery
of the seating area; the girls give angry glares. This is *their*
band—everyone else, go away.

The song ends with a gusty WHOOOOO! from the girls.
Their cheers die down, replaced by the soft whirr of the
generators, trying to pump some air into the beer dog.

But nothing is as forlorn as Machinery Hill. On a sunny
day you'd have the stone-faced farmers making their stoic
appraisal, city people clambering into the cabs and pretend-
ing they were gathering the wealth of the fields. Today the
bright machinery sits alone like pieces of artillery abandoned
in a hasty retreat.

A few of the machines manage to show some dignity. The
threshers and bailers look like brainless automatons, and the
tractors and earthmovers have the look of oxen who endure
the rain with unblinking forbearance. The combines, however, have a certain nobility to them. With their wide steel
jaw and thick body, they look like dinosaurs bent down to
graze. You can imagine them rearing up on their back legs
and stomping off. Left alone in the rain, the combines look
as though they are simply napping. Climb up in the cab if
you wish, but tread softly.

The combines, of course, are instruments of harvest, machines that gather up summer and leave stubble for winter
to cover. The combines have been running in the fields for
some time now; summer is fading away. The day's rain was
a cold rain, a greeting card from autumn.

The sun came out at three that day, and it was warm

enough for tank tops. Eventually the dog stood up and took his tongue out of the dirt. The Poncho People removed their tarpaulins. Newcomers looked up at the clearing sky and smiled, as though this had been arranged for their benefit. The rides started up again, the Midway shaking itself dry like a great and gaudy beast, and the fair sat back to bask in the light of fall's first day.

5

Final Notes

I thought this year's ad campaign was a little weak. Last year, if I recall correctly, they had an illustration of happy barnyard animals waving, presumably inviting us to come by and say hello before they're shoved into the abattoir for our pleasure. This year's campaign made the appeal to the senses, as though we're all jaded libertines in need of some new jolts. FEEEEEEEL IT! said the billboards. TAAAAASTE IT! SMELLLLLL IT!

They left out the obvious ones: STEPPPPPP IN IT! PAAAAAY FOR IT! ELLLLLLLBOW SOMEONE IN THE BACK! Of course, you might wonder why the fair needs to advertise at all. It's not like anyone sees the billboards and says, "What? A *fair?* I thought last year was a one-shot deal!" All they needed were three billboards: FAIR SOON for the week before, FAIR NOW when it was on, and FAIR DONE when it was over.

I don't know about you, but I'm ready for the FAIR DONE sign. I know that's heresy; the fair is our last bulwark against fall, and once it's over, thirty-five feet of snow immediately blankets the city. Fine with me. SHIIIIIVER IN IT! I say. I have simply gone to the fair too many times. Once is a delight; you come away stuffed and dizzy. But make Mahatma Gandhi and Mother Teresa go seven times, find parking, fight the crowds, attempt to locate a restroom that is not hip deep in the pubic hair of strangers, and they end the day rolling around in the sawdust, trying to gouge each other's eyes out.

Not everything I've seen has made it into the paper. Yet. Here are some leftover observations from the fair of 1989.

Most Inspiring Moment: a man wearing a cap that says, "From Wine, Women, and Song to Beer, the Old Lady, and TV," examines a wooden plaque that says, "Wine, Women, and Walleyes," and looks as though there are new worlds to explore after all.

Best Midway Prize That Somehow Says It All: a ceramic teddy bear riding a unicorn.

Most Dubious Honor: in the Education Building, the Community Colleges' booth has a computer quiz to test your knowledge of obscure outstate educational institutions. If you answer every question incorrectly, as I did, you are rewarded with a screen that says, CONGRATULATIONS! YOU ARE NOW AN HONORARY ALUMNUS OF MINNESOTA COMMUNITY COLLEGES. Another guy taking the quiz on the machine next to me finished when I did and got the same degree. We threw our caps in the air and embraced, having gone through so much together and knowing our lives were about to take different directions, but promising to keep in touch.

I passed it off as a joke, but last Friday I received my loan payment booklet. It made me wish I'd taken the quiz at the Vo-Tech booth, where at least the screen says, CONGRATULATIONS! YOU MAY NOW BEGIN TO DEFAULT ON YOUR LOANS.

Most Incomprehensible Excuse for Drawing a Crowd: demonstrations. Put down thirty chairs and have someone start speaking, and it'll be standing-room-only. The topic is always "Sulfur: the Homemaker's Friend" or something equally riveting. Doesn't matter. Arrange the chairs and people will appear.

But the Beef Theater was perhaps the worst. I wandered into the Beef Theater expecting to see an all-Guernsey version of *Waiting for Godot,* or maybe a method actor who had spent innumerable hours on four legs staring impassively at a fence. What I saw was a ten-minute commercial for the beef industry, the sort of thing they air on Sunday afternoons after football season is over. Only not as exciting.

Most Disillusioning Moment: watching the cow judging at the Coliseum and realizing that, just like the Miss America pageant, they probably don't give much weight to the essay portion of the contest here, either.

Best Surprise Appearance by a Slain but Still Controversial Figure: a portrait of Malcolm X, done entirely in seeds. He was in the Crop Art Gallery, along with Willie Nelson, Bill Cosby, and Einstein. "What do they have in common?" I asked an observer. "Well, they're all done in seeds," he replied.

Most Revolting Example of Nature: Cal the boar, winner of the largest hog competition. Cal weighed in at 1,020 pounds, roughly 940 pounds of which was testicles. When Cal dies he will be reincarnated as a guy who spends his entire night on the Midway hurling softballs at beer bottles.

Worst Realization: that you have been eating with the same hand you used to pet Cal the boar.

Worst Sight I Wish I Hadn't Seen: a woman in sweat pants passed out open-mouthed in a Vibrating Chair, with a Vibrating Chair salesperson running a vibrating suction cup around her jaw. She was, no doubt, FEEEEEELING IT.

Worst Social Scourge Not Appearing at the Fair, Although You Almost Expected to See It: Deep-Fried Crack, or Crack-on-a-Stick.

Most Ominous Sign of Rural Sadism: in the 4-H Building, the Steele chapter's booth had a display with a massive branding iron in the shape of the 4-H logo, resting on a bed of coals. I asked someone if this was used on initiates, and he said no, absolutely *not,* that's just a rumor. But I followed him around for a while and noted that he walked with a curious hitch, and *he never sat down.*

These are only some of the curiosities. I'm sure I'd have seen more if I'd stayed all day, sunup to sundown. But after too many trips, the fair begins to resemble the Calcutta of Fun. You want to get away from the crowds, back to a world where people park on the streets instead of the lawn, sit down when they eat, carry purses instead of plastic bags from water-purifier manufacturers. A world where no one is carrying a four-foot stuffed animal that looks like it fell out of someone's acid trip.

That, of course, is the real purpose of the State Fair.

It makes the real world look good.

Riding the Whistle

When the paper sent me to New York to do a story, I insisted on taking the train. The last time I flew to New York, I was so utterly terrorized by turbulence I had to sit in the passenger lobby for an hour, quivering like a Lutheran dessert, before I could stand and leave the terminal. I'd only survived the return trip by drinking myself into a moronic stupor. This, I decided, would never happen again.

But the train, with sleeping car, was twice the cost of an airline ticket. To justify the expense, I had to write about the experience, and here is the result. A few notes: the last few times I've taken the train, the food's been better. They've brought back linen and china. And at least twice I've found myself on a car called the Pacific Queen, the same one I write about below. I always end up in the same room: Number Seven. Mysterious creatures, these trains.

The following, I think, is typical. I took a sleeping-car train to New York City, following the old routes, living the old rhythms the jets have tried to kill. The experience taught me three things: one, the trains aren't dead. They're coming back. Rarely on time, granted, but coming back nonetheless. Two, I never want to go over a high bridge in a train again in my life. Three, there's no trip like a train trip. That says a lot for jets, actually. But it says more for the trains.

St. Paul to Chicago; Coach

"But what if someone puts a penny on the tracks?" the guy across the aisle whines. He has a voice best suited to walking up to your table and announcing that he would be your waiter tonight. "What if we derail?"

This is not likely. Put a penny on the tracks, let a train pass over it, and you have a thin penny. What is more likely is that I will take the hard little pillow Amtrak provides for my comfort and hold it down over this guy's face until he quiets down, for he has been blathering on without cease since we left. Compounding matters are two oversugared tots who amused themselves by jumping up and down in front of strangers and demanding that you guess the names of their cousin. Sample dialogue:

"Starts with X!"

"Xavier."

"No!"

"To hell with you, kid."

It is eight hours to Chicago, and it feels like one interminable taxi down a runway in a plane never taking off. The tracks are in such bad shape that the train has to tiptoe through most of Wisconsin. Go ahead, put a penny on the rails. It'll double their maintenance budget. I have a headache and I miss my wife and let's just not talk about this leg of the trip.

Chicago

We change in Chicago, the town known on occasion to toddle. The train station was built in 1926, and that also appears to have been the last time it was swept or painted. I drag my belongings to the baggage department and show them which bag contains the breakables, so they won't have to waste energy throwing all my bags around with careless velocity. As I have had nothing to eat but my cuticles—the train was late and I feared missing my connection—I purchase a small, boiled mailing tube masquerading as a hot dog, slather it with red mucilage and wolf it down. My comfort thus assured, I look for a place in the station where I can sit down and get up without sticking to my chair.

I spent my layover in Amtrak's First Class Lounge, where the lure, apparently, is hearing a better class of baby wail its lungs out. The lounge looks like a dentist's office, circa 1959; in the center is a gnarled tree cowering under a blast of fluorescent light; in one corner, a TV bolted high on the wall in the mode favored by mental institutions.

To my left sits an old man. He has reached the age when pants naturally crawl up to the sternum, and he wears a hat mashed down on his head. He studies the room in silence for ten minutes, then says to no one in particular, "Maybe the money is going into improving the tracks."

There is no information board in the lounge to tell you when your train is due, the gate from which it departs, whether it even exists. You have to depend on your Amtrak employee. They're not hard to identify—all wear uniforms left over from some cocktail lounge's attempt to commemorate the Bicentennial. But the depot is not exactly overrun with them. When you find one, the wisest thing to do is to nail his feet to the floor and charge other passengers a fee to speak with him. When half the Coach Class waiting room rose and shuffled out, I actually found one of the scarce, uniquely attired individuals and inquired if they were boarding the train to New York. They were. I schlepped my bags down to the tracks, got in line, stepped through the gate—

Chicago to New York via Sleeper
—I step through the gate, and something changes. There is a blast of cool air with the tang of diesel; the train stretches ahead into the distance, engines throbbing. This isn't the train that takes you to your connection; this is the train that takes you all the way to where you want to go, the train that was waiting for you all this time.

My car was called the Pacific Queen, a refurbished sleeper

built in 1948 but looking new and polished. There is a slight trouble boarding when everyone attempts to get into the car at the same time, a feat equal in ease to shoving cashew nuts down a funnel. The hallway of the car is wide enough for two people to pass if one of them doesn't show up. Unfortunately, between me and my room stood an adherent of the Pavarotti diet. How he was going to get through his cabin door without the help of grease, good will, and a battering ram, no one knew. But I try to pass him. We perform a little dance. He glares at me for having the gall to be average weight for my height. I slip past, winded, and find my room; I drop my baggage, slide the door shut, and look around.

It doesn't take long to look around the room. Six feet long, three feet wide, eight feet tall. A coffin with great headroom. The rooms are masterpieces of economy—every square inch serves a function. The sink folds into the wall. The bed folds into the wall. You're surprised the wall doesn't fold into the wall. You've one comfortable seat, and a personal commode. The important items, like the reading lights and the ashtrays, are located at a height accessible from the seat and the bed. Everything is painted a regrettable shade of beige, but the novelty and echoes of a past era are so pronounced you expect a butler to be lying prone on the bed when you pull it down.

There are men in the corridors, all wearing spoiled-cranberry-colored Amtrak jackets, talking into walkie-talkies and getting furtive crackles in response. I suspect they are telling the engineer that the majority of the people on the train are standing up, and hence, this would be a good time for the train to lurch forward and knock everyone back into their seats. The engineer apparently agrees; the train shudders and coughs, the wheels squeal, and the train begins its halting pull out of the station.

We were still chugging through Chicago when my porter delivered the first-class amenities. These included a packet of stationery, a small bottle of wine, and the famed Amtrak Snack Pack, which contains everything from French cheese to a Slim Jim. I am given my meal vouchers—first-class tickets include free meals—but that, as we are about to see, is not exactly an act of charity.

Dinner

They seat you European Style, which is a fancy term for Forced to Eat with Strangers. My table companion this evening is an engineer from Illinois who sells drill bits to the Japanese. He has not only participated in the drilling of huge tunnels, he has done so without getting a single interesting anecdote from the experience.

The menu describes the food as though it were a gourmet's dream, and the waiters serve it with fabulous cheer. If I were the waiters, I would serve it and hide. Here, alas, is food that makes you wish you were on an airplane. Microwaves are the culprit. The New York strip tastes like a horse's bit; the cheeseburger had all the aroma and flavor of particle board. The meatless manicotti looks less like a meal than a murder scene.

The coffee is good. You have to fire signal flares to get a second cup, but it is hot and tasty—two adjectives not found in close proximity to one another in the Amtrak kitchen. The days of white linen tablecloths and china are gone, and where once the dining car was an oasis of civility, it is now a forced-labor camp. There's no escape. You can't order out. The general attitude was best expressed by one waiter's reply to a customer's attempted substitution.

"The cook," he said, "don't make no alternations." Bingo.

The Bar Car, or Death Stops at Toledo

In the double-decker cars, the bar car is a downstairs, giving it the air of a speakeasy. The chairs face each other, encouraging confabulation. East of the Mississippi, the car is a strange beast—a long bar in the middle of the car, a few rows of seats pointed toward the front. Everyone sits in a chair, drinking, looking forward. It looks like an audience waiting for its hallucination to show up and take the stage. There are two businessmen, hovering like zeppelins around the mooring post of a solitary blond woman. They are talking

and telling jokes, and she, to their delight, is laughing in all
the right places.

We also have a crazy on board, a genuine, goat-scented
bozo muttering a long and rambling account of his dispute
with the White House. It seemed to be a matter of money
and a lack of respect.

"So I call the president. And he gets mad if you can b'lieve
that, says it's a bad day, can I call him later. Well. Well well,
I've had enough."

I turn to the blond in the seat across the aisle, jerk a thumb
at the mutterer.

"Uh . . ." she says, "some people are different." I am
about to nod agreement, but she continues: "I mean, I'm
pretty bizarre myself."

"You are bizarre," says one of the businessmen, "but I
mean that in a positive sense."

Well well, I've had enough. I go back to the bar. Our
bartender tonight is named Nick, a twitchy sliver of a man
with a laugh that sounds like a hacksaw working on a metal
pole. There is a sign over the bar that reads ASK TO HEAR
OUR TRAIN WHISTLE. I ask.

"There's no whistle," says Nick. "I just reach under the
bar and make like I'm pressing something. I say, 'You hear
that?'; and they say, 'Yeah . . . yeah, I do.' " Nick shakes
his head. "The things I do to amuse myself."

I ask Nick what sorts of things he has seen working this
bar.

"Life, death, you name it." Death? "New Year's Eve,
three guys had a heart attack here in the bar. While we were
stopped in Toledo."

An older couple with grave Slavic faces have come in to
order vodka; death they understand. They pay attention.
Particularly since Toledo happens to be our next stop.

"A guy had a heart attack as we were pullin' in. Nothing
much you can do but keep him comfortable. I closed the bar,
but you always got the morbidites walking over the body and
saying, 'Ya gotta beer?' " He frowns. "We radioed ahead,
there was an ambulance waiting. Just as they're rollin' him

off, another guy kicks. Had to get the ambulance back for him. Half an hour later, we're pulling out of town, another one gets it. Had to stop again to pull him off."

A conductor comes through to catch the end of Nick's disquisition on the way of all flesh.

"New Year's Eve?" he asks. Nick nods. The conductor looks around the bar as if to tell us not to even think about having a heart attack. Then he announces that we're pulling into Toledo.

"Wha we doin' in Toledo?" shouts one of the businessmen from the darkened bar. His voice sounds like red meat and Winstons.

"No one," says his buddy, "shoul' live in Toledo." The blonde laughs; Nick shrugs.

Good Night

I undress in my room. I realize that I cannot take the bed down without standing outside in the corridor, so I put my clothes back on. I do not want people to come by and see me naked, wrestling with a wall. The bed comes down with a clunk; I climb up, slide the doors closed, undress with something less than the grace of a snake shedding a skin, and stow my clothes in the closet. I put my shoes in the shoe locker—which, as my porter reminded me, was accessible from the hallway, so I'd best not put anything valuable there. I had wondered why my shoe locker was open to the world, when I realize that in the old days the porters came by and shined your shoes while you slept. My porter hadn't mentioned that. Of course, I'm sure in the heyday of trains they didn't go around slinging out Slim Jims with abandon, either.

I get into bed. It's not bad—imagine a very thick doctor's examining table hooked up to the World's Largest Magic Fingers machine, and you have a bed on a moving train. I like the idea of hurtling headfirst toward New York City at 95 mph, on my stomach, riding this arrow fired at the heart of Manhattan. If we have a crash, of course, my socks and my brains will be indistinguishable. I take off the covers and remove my socks, just to prevent confusion.

But a crash is my last worry; or anyone else's, probably. A train at night on good tracks feels like a beast running for the sheer pleasure of running surefooted over favorite terrain.

And a train at night cradles you, rocks you back and forth. The familiar clack and slap of wheels against the rail marks the miles and the minutes, until neither matters and you are ushered gently into smooth slumber.

The last thing you hear before you sleep is the whistle, the most haunting sound ever made by man. If that sound came from a wild animal, primitive man would have ascribed great wisdom and sadness to it, and he would have feared it. We know what a train whistle is when we hear it, but we don't know what it means. No one can hear it without feeling the sudden thrust of melancholy against the heart: something is passing by, going to where I am not.

It doesn't feel any different when you're on the train, riding the whistle; then it speaks of the places you are passing and leaving, not the places you are heading toward. But the emotion on both sides fades with the whistle. The sound opens the air and lets the train behind it stitch it back together again. Behind you the gates swing up and traffic lumbers over the rails. By the time you wake up, the train will have made a neat and seamless suture of all the land you traveled while you slept, and if you dreamed of the whistle, it will be part of the dream you can never quite fit into words.

Toppling into the River

Breakfast looks like something for which you would blame your dog. I am playing a game with my eggs: I swallow them and they want to come back up. It is a frisky and playful thing, this breakfast. It doesn't help matters that we appear to be approximately three inches from falling into the Hudson. The train is barreling along at a disconcerting angle, taking turns I am certain are going to dunk us into the drink. I begin to feel the sensation I used to get on planes before I swore off flying—the feeling of one anxious rat gnawing on the rope that holds closed the cage containing hundreds of anxious rats. I tell myself that this is crazy.

I do not know, of course, that on the way home, on a different train that threads a thin path along a mountain in West Virginia my steward will confess to a horror of the route. "Derailed the last time," he will say. "The train just hung there. I thought we were going to go down the hill and into the river." I don't know this yet, and I think I'm being silly for entertaining thoughts of derailing.

Derailing. It doesn't sound so bad, really; planes CRASH, a word that sounds like it probably feels. But "derailing" sounds almost civilized. *Pahrdon, sahr, but we will be derailing at eight, if you would care to join us.*

But we are running right along the banks of the Hudson, and I am a little unnerved. Prior to our certain gurgling demise, however, we are at least treated to scenery. Old bridges, full of rough and ugly grace; houses built high on bluffs; a ruined castle on an island. This is old America, and the land no longer looks as though it has grudgingly agreed to be civilized. We are soon joined by other tracks, and suburban train stations appear. The posters advertise the New York that is just an hour away.

I go back to my cabin and watch the world slide by. Like most trains, the Lake Shore Express crawls in through the back door of the city, making a slow, clanking trip through the industrial section. We see old factories, abandoned warehouses, ramshackle homes with backyards full of all sorts of urban flotsam. There's much colorful, incomprehensible graffiti, like the remains of an ancient culture that reached its peak with the Magic Marker Age. Then the city disappears. Completely disappears. And we are in hell.

Hell, in this case, is an eternal tunnel caked with soot, dimly lit, ancient. The presence of small pools of light tells you that this is a place in New York so bad that no one will come down here to steal the light bulbs. Tracks are visible on either side of the train as far as the dim light permits me to see, and I hear a faint groaning of wheels and tired steel.

Up above, my porter tells me, is sunshine, and Manhattan.

The train slows, the wheels cry, we stop. A voice cries, "Grand Central Station," just like it ought to be. I step off into a blast of cool air, flavored with urine. My porter hands me my bags. "They used to roll out the red carpet for the Twentieth Century Limited," he notes. But it's bare concrete all the way to the stairs. I thank him, pick up my luggage and struggle toward the exit, miles down the platform. Up the stairs, up a ramp, past people with the grim New York look of great and indifferent importance, that lemming-with-an-MBA look. They bump into my baggage with extra zeal.

Upstairs is Grand Central Station, newly polished and painted. I put down my bags and look up at that magnificent ceiling. The ceiling, unlike the abstract heights airplanes reach, is high enough to dazzle and awe. If you could jump as high as it makes you feel, you could touch it. I look like a tourist, I know, standing there looking up, mouth probably slack with a rube's salute. But I don't live here. I can do that. That's the whole point of the trip—to ride a narrow box across the country and be spilled into a room whose height outreaches every dream of height you've had on the train. If people walking by want to snicker at the hick, well, I have earned this.

This trip had started in the Midwest, at a place where trains merely stopped; it ends where trains had begun, at a place where trains have always mattered. There was nothing of home left in me by now—the motion of the train had shook home out of me a long time before.

But it put something else in its place, something besides miles. When I lay down to sleep in my hotel room, I could still feel the rhythm of the train, as if I were still riding the rapids of that long metal river. The train ebbs from your blood slowly, leaving just an aftertaste of the whistle and the iron. You savor that taste until you board a train again.

The Bronx Is Up and the Battery's Down, Although Assault Is Going Through the Roof

NEW YORK, EVER THE CITADEL OF FRIENDLINESS AND HOSpitality, sends someone out to meet you when you show up. Unfortunately, this person is a thief.

I had not been in Manhattan for four minutes when a toothless lump of stubble and bones hobbled up to me and offered to get me a cab. I had encountered this scam before. He would ask me for a deposit on the cab, which would, through bum's alchemy, be converted into Night Train wine the moment he was out of my sight. Or he would lead me around the corner to his crack-starved confederates who traffic in stolen travel irons, and they would hack me into fodder for the next day's tabloid headlines. HICK SLAIN IN CAB SCAM MAYHEM.

I told him no. He was insistent. I ignored him. He leaned close, his breath so rank it made my fillings rust over, and said he'd give me discount rates. Finally I dropped my bags, and did the one thing New Yorkers understand: I yelled.

"Yo! Do I look like I just got off the (insert colorful Brooklyn-accented profanity here) boat?"

He looked at me with narrowed eyes. There I was, standing outside a train station, asking him if I looked like I had gotten off a boat. Clearly, I was crazier than he was. He slunk back into the shadows and left me alone.

That's how you deal with New Yorkers. If they yell, yell louder. If they honk, honk louder. The city gives you a shove? Shove it back. It's a braying, seething, teeth-grinding Mixmaster of humanity, and the setting is always on puree. How anyone can get up every day and knock back their ration of that fetid cocktail is a mystery to me; after three days on that benighted sliver of land I was so hungry for midwestern geniality I was breaking into tears at the Garrison Keillor displays in the bookstores. The following vignettes are scenes from daily Manhattan life, presented to dissuade you from ever going there. I'd say these stories are the written equivalent of sawhorses with blinking lights, but that would mean someone would steal them during the night.

Before you think these are the damaged mewings of a timid small-town stripling, trust me: I used to love New York. I once thought it was the greatest city on earth.

Then I went there.

The Messenger of Death

New York traffic is eternally congested. During rush hour, which is generally defined as the period of time in which the sun is visible, driving around town is like holding a foot race in a tar pit. Often the fastest way to get across the city is to die and be reincarnated, ideally in the body of someone who stands to inherit a rent-controlled apartment. The subways are well and good (see Stinking Tunnels of Danger, below) but they are not as fast as the bicycle. Only bicycle messengers can slide through the streets at high speeds. They have no fear of death. I'm serious—they really don't care if they kill you.

Bicycle messengers are fundamentally decent people; they have the number 911 imbedded in the tread of their bikes, so after they have blown through an intersection like a howitzer shell fired into a down pillow, you can read the tire marks on their victims and know who to call for medical assistance. But in some small way, you cheer them on—

they're a paper cut in the lumbering mass of the city, a molecule of mercury sluicing through the rusted gutters of the street. They *are* the last free spirits on the roads, and you're glad they're around.

Until one of the bastards knocks you down.

I was standing on a typical midtown street. Approximately 47,293 people were clustered on the corner, waiting for the light. When it changed from DON'T YOU WALK NOW to GOWAN, GET OUTTA HERE, I waited for the traffic to clear, then stepped into the street. Alone. The other 47,292 people stayed behind. As practiced New Yorkers, they knew to pause for the additional 0.06 seconds on the chance a bicycle messenger was flying their way. Hick that I am, I walked right into the path of the messenger.

If he had hit me dead on, I wouldn't be here today. I'd be slouched on Fifth Avenue with a tin cup and a sign that read PARALYZED BY BIKE MESSENGER. PLEASE HELP. He hit me in the satchel I carry, bounced off, and skidded into the intersection. I was knocked backwards by the force of the collision, but fell into the 47,292 people who were now moving off the curb, and who buoyed me forward. People from both curbs flowed around the prostrate messenger, who waited until the pedestrians passed, then stood up, shook the asphalt out of his hair, picked up his bike and continued on *without even looking in my direction.*

I felt better knowing that somewhere out there, there was the large and inflexible rear end of a hastily breaking bus with his name on it. And it comforted me to know that fax technology is making him obsolete. Soon New Yorkers won't have to worry about bike messengers. Although I understand that in order to preserve local New York color, fax manufacturers have developed a machine that leaps from its place and hits you in the teeth.

I Am Not Crazy. The Men from Venus Told Me So.

The week before I arrived, a man had charged through the streets waving a knife until surrounded by cops. The police, acting in accordance with the recently passed Do the

World a Favor Act, shot the man dead. MIDTOWN MACHETE MAYHEM was the *New York Post*'s headline the next day. The story described the man as "crazed." Not crazy, mind you: crazed.

The distinction has merit in New York. Using the word crazy raises the ire of the groups like the National Association for the Crazy, who fear New Yorkers will get a bad image of crazy people. "You always hear about the machete-wielding maniacs," they protest. "You never hear about the ones dedicated to pointing out that the CIA uses robot dogs to spy on us."

Nevertheless, there *are* crazy people in New York. I met two. The first was right outside the Cuban consulate—a well-dressed man who accosted all passersby and demanded to know if they were talking to him. "Are you talking to me?" he said, to each who passed. He looked furious, as though he was being forced by inner demons to recite *Taxi Driver* dialogue and found the whole thing utterly predictable. "Look at me!" his expression seemed to be saying. "Mad as a rabbit jackal, and can't even think of my own lines!"

As he headed my way, I wondered what I would say. "No, I'm not talking to you" would be accurate, but since I would have to talk to him to say it, the contradiction might permanently fuse his brain, and he would stand there for years like the Tin Woodman, synapses rusted. "Yes, I am talking to you" might confirm that I was Boab, sixth son of Satan, come to smite him, and then he'd haul out the machete. CUBAN CONSULATE CUT-FEST, the papers would say. When he passed me, spitting out his dialogue, I merely whistled a merry tune. Something from the knife-fight scene in *West Side Story,* I think.

The second crazy person was in Union Square. He was engaged in civic work, pointing out to everyone the various components of The Big Picture. He would walk up to a wastebasket, point a skinny digit at it, and say, "That is part of The Big Picture." Then he'd wheel around, cite each of the columns on a bank façade, and announce that each was part of The Big Picture. I watched him until he knelt at a splatter of pigeon excreta and announced that it, too, was part of, well, you know. I had a cruel desire to walk over and dump a box of rice in front of him and see if he would address the rice individually or stand back and say, "The rice, taken as a whole, is part of The Big Picture."

When I left him, he was heading north, toward midtown, where all the corporations are headquartered. If some executive passes him and sees him look skyward with reverence and intone, "Chemical Bank is part of The Big Picture," he'd probably be hired on the spot as a long-range planner. True visionaries are rare.

The Deli from Beyond the River Styx

I stay at the same hotel each time I visit, and always on the seventh floor. That's where they always put me. I have come to believe that the rest of the hotel does not exist, and that 708 and 709, the only rooms I have had in six visits, are the only rooms in the hotel. Every other room is filled with concrete. That explains the cost of the room. I don't complain about the high price because I know they would shrug, smile, and say, But, sir, taxes on this building are so very high, and seeing as all our rooms but two are filled with concrete, we must make our money where we can. I do not mind, because I always look right into the same office across the street, and I note with pleasure that every year it is occupied by a different person. Either it is the office given to those on the way up, or it's where the company chooses to dump people it's going to fire.

If I'd have known six years ago that I'd always look into the same window, I would have put on a sheet, doused it with ketchup, waited until the occupant of the office looked my way, then staggered around my room like a murdered spirit that knows no rest. I'd do this every year until the lore got around and every occupant of that office spent their days nervously looking across the street at 708. Then this last trip out I'd have arranged an interview with the person in that office, and at the right moment, looked out the window and clutched my throat. When the occupant of the office looked across the street, saw nothing, and asked me what was the matter, I'd say, "Nothing, nothing, it's just . . . just that my brother was murdered in that room."

But, stupid me, I neglected to start this in motion, and next time I may get another room—the hotel is under renovation. They have in the lobby the new floor plans, the building permits, and the receipts from the Mafia authorizing construction, so next time I might be one of the presently fictitious floors. But no matter what room they stick me in, I will still be in the thrall of the Cruelest Deli on Earth. The Bunny Deli.

The Bunny Deli ("Third World Service at First World Prices!") is the only twenty-four-hour deli in the area, and as such it is the only place local hotel guests can go for staples. The nearby hotels, which include the Waldorf-Astoria and the Lexington, seem to have clienteles that consist entirely of Germans unfamiliar with the exchange rate; whenever I go to the Bunny at night, all I hear are cheerful Teutons saying, "Ja, ja," as they count out seven traveler's checks for a carton of milk and a paper. Perhaps they are nostalgic for Weimar-era prices. *"Vas ist das?* Four tousand dollars for der apple und der postcard? Gretel! Get der wheelbarrow mit der money, ha ha ha!"

I was at the mercy of the Bunny when I checked into my hotel. It was late at night, and nothing was open. The Bunny stood on the corner, lit up and blazing like a tourism office for Hell. I had no choice. I shouldered my way past a knot of happy Germans and examined the buffet. Eight bins of various unidentifiable Korean dishes. I avoided anything that looked like breaded puppy hindquarters, a Korean staple, and filled my plate with rice and chicken. I avoided the pungent Korean specialty, kimchi, since there was a notice in my hotel room prohibiting the exhalation of kimchi fumes in the room, as it is hard on the woodwork. After I had piled up a mound of food, I took it to the counter.

"THIS IT?" shouted the clerk. I nodded; she picked up my tray, dumped it on a scale and announced a fabulous sum. I had apparently chosen the Gold 'n' Cocaine Fried

Rice. I paid, grabbed a few packets of soy sauce and headed toward the seating area upstairs.

"HEY!" called the clerk. "HEY! SOY SAUCE EXTRA!" I turned. Soy sauce *extra*? In America, land of free condiments? What else would I be charged for—deep breaths? Use of the door, wear and tear on the cash register?

I paid for my soy and went upstairs. It was deserted. I took a seat, unfurled my *New York Times,* and started to shovel in the Airedale medley or the Schnauzer rolls or whatever I had ordered, when an employee cleaning tables pointed out that booths were reserved for four or more people. I pointed out that the place was only slightly more populated than Grant's Tomb. The clerk was adamant. I moved to a table.

It goes without saying that I had heartburn that night. I had no antacids. I could hear the neon sign of the Bunny Deli clicking on and off all night, and I knew they'd be open if I wanted to get something to relieve my misery.

I wouldn't give them the satisfaction.

Now you know what I went through. Bad food at high prices, crazy folk roaming the streets, ten-speed executioners. You understand why I was happy to leave. New Yorkers certainly couldn't understand my reaction. They thrive on the stuff. They are the type of people who, if struck by a bus and carried fifty feet, will feel they got the better of the deal because they didn't pay the fare.

Such a person was the young woman who stood behind me in the line for the train out of town. We fell to talking, and I dragged out my grievances. She didn't understand a word I was saying. So I unholstered the big guns. I told her I lived next to a lake. (I lied.) What I paid in rent. What houses cost. How the streets were clean and uncluttered. How the gentle folk lived in peace and harmony (I left out the skinheads down the block). She either thought me mad or was horrified to learn that maybe, just maybe, there was a place on earth better than N.Y.C. When she excused herself and ran to her car, I watched her go with pity.

I boarded the car bound for Minnesota. I returned my wallet to my back pocket, no longer worried about thieves. And I relaxed. I was going home. Back to the good, sane land I loved. I lit a cigarette and began to think of the fair green lands beyond.

"Excuse me." I opened my eyes to see a blond, blue-eyed man in a flannel shirt, leaning across the aisle. "*This* is the *non*-smoking section."

I stubbed out my cigarette. I was bound for Minnesota, all right. Somewhere in the bowels of the Bunny Deli they were lighting up, breathing deep, and laughing.

Another Needless Survey
of Beers

━━

AVOID ALL BEERS WITH A MONK ON THE LABEL. I LEARNED
this several years ago when I invested $3.25 in a Belgian
indignity called St. Sixtus. The label had a fat, laughing
monk; evidently, the beer was being marketed toward that
highly coveted market of celibate, devout, easily amused
beer drinkers.

It was the vilest thing I ever tasted. If you stuffed yeast in
your rain gutters, left it there for six months and then used
the mixture to strain roofing tar, you'd have St. Sixtus. A
unique, *chewy* beer. That was the last time I paid a lot of
money for beer. Why, I decided, pay $3.25 for one bottle of
beer when you can get twelve bottles for the same price? I
became a connoisseur of cheap beer, friend to the common
can. No slight to people who enjoy the fine products described above, but I'd rather be content with Proletarian Swill
than go without because the bar doesn't serve Dortlander
Pilsner Van Urquell Di Somoza Lager Ale. My motto: "I've
had worse."

Naturally, I was the choice to conduct our first annual
Review of Cheap Beers. The event was held at a friend's
house; shortly after I showed up, bearing a clanking sack of

industrial sedative, my host pulled an expensive, obscure beer from the fridge.

"You need a control beer," he said. "Something good." He handed me a bottle of something German—Anschluss Special, or Esser du Goebbels, I can't remember. "I got this today. Buck and a quarter a bottle." I looked at the label, and there he was. The Monk. Grinning. This was going to be fun.

I had chosen my cheap beers with care, judging them on the basis by which true beer fans rank their favorites: attractiveness of can (Jacob Best), ease with which the label can be peeled off intact (Schmidt's), local sentimental favorite (Gluek's), cheapness (Milwaukee's Best), and novelty (Harley-Davidson beer, $1.69 a six-pack). In addition to the Monk beer, I served a glass which consisted of all the cheap beers, poured together and stirred. A bowl of nacho chips was set out, so the participants could clear their palates between sips.

The testers consisted of Rich, the host who had given me the obscure German beer; Steve, who doesn't like beer but would date any of the women in the beer commercials, particularly those for Michelob Dry; and Wesley, who regards beer as no more than a rough draft for Scotch. Differ as they may in their affection for beer, all are men, and all men secretly believe they *know beer*. I told them that one of the beers before them was an expensive German beer, and the rest were cheap. They had to spot the Monk.

Rich went first. He tasted all the beers but the mixed concoction, and pronounced that I had poured the same beer into every glass. Then he cleared his palate and retraced his steps. The expensive German beer, he said, had "a metallic taste—like there were filings in the bottom of the keg." Three other beers were dismissed as being insubstantial, but the Harley-Davidson beer earned high marks for potency. Asked to choose which was the German, and hence the top-of-the-line, he chose the Harley-Davidson beer. I was faced with having to tell him that what he thought the $1.25-per-bottle beer was actually the $1.69-per-six-pack brand. This would crush his illusions. I couldn't wait.

Steve dismissed all the beers, and had particular scorn for the Harley brand, which he called "beery." Strong words. Trading on his years of watching people pay good money for St. Sixtus and related brands, he said that the Harley beer was "probably supposed to be the best, but I think it stinks." He had a kind word for Milwaukee Light, praising its lack of aftertaste: "After you drink it, you can forget about it quicker."

Wesley also picked Harley beer as the German brand, praising its body and calling it "distinctive." The German beer earned curt disdain: "The least flavor of all of them."

All were unanimous on the mixed beer: it was awful.

"Is this the Harley beer?" asked Rich.

"This must be really expensive," said Steve.

Wesley just stared at his glass, alarmed.

The winners, in case you're interested: local favorite Schmidt's, followed by Jacob Best, the German beer, Gluek, and Milwaukee's Best. I wasn't surprised by Schmidt's strong showing; it is archetypal beer. Neither good nor bad, it just *is*. What pleased me most was the general consensus that Harley-Davidson, the worst-tasting of the batch, was regarded as being the most expensive.

This tell you anything?

It tells me that people really want to drink cheap beer, but fall prey to their own egos. Most beer has—shudder—working-class connotations; upper-class beer drinkers want a brew that says, "You do not work with your hands." One way to achieve this is to drink something foreign. Never mind if the name of the beer translates as "The Favorite of Beet-Eating Steamfitters"; if the label is ornate and has another language on it, so much the better.

The second method is to drink undrinkable beers. The day I bought the beers for the Cheap Beer Taste Test, I stood in line by a gentleman buying Guiness Stout and Foster's Lager. Now, I buy Guiness on occasion; I find it restores luster and shine to my wood furniture, and smeared around the front door, it keeps the dogs away. Foster's is fine, and is a favorite in Australia, particularly by people who point out with pride that Australia was founded as a penal colony. This gentleman paid $13.00 for his twelve bottles—exactly what I paid for thirty cans of cheap beer. He looked miserable—aw, Christ, another joyless weekend of warm, viscous beer—but he also looked at my purchases with scorn. His look said it all: *I bet you bowl, too.*

Well, to hell with him. If you would like to investigate cheap beers, try the ones listed above, or sample these favorites. Each deserves its own award, and I have provided them:

Best Beer to Drink If You're Working Up the Courage to Rob a Convenience Store: Country Club, from the Pearl Brewery of San Antonio. Three bucks for a six-pack of half-quart cans. Suggested slogan: "What'll You Have—Besides What's in the Till?"

Most Scarred Bottles per Case: a toss-up between Hamm's and Schell's. Both appear to have hurled their bottles into a ravine and chosen the bottles that survived intact. Hamm's gets extra points for using ripped labels.

Most Life-Threatening Bottles: Schmidt's Big Mouth. If Honeywell made the cap for the Big Mouth, there would be protesters at the gates every day, for the saloons run red with the blood spilled by this hellish device. It is impossible to open a Big Mouth without drawing blood. First you jam your finger in a ring the diameter of a capillary vessel, and then you pull up, severing your finger at the tip; this action exposes several strips of sharp, glinting metal, on which you promptly flay a knuckle to the bone. Then you leave the cap sitting on the table, so you can drive your fist into it when pounding the table to make a point. Perhaps Schmidt's will next bring out a special, limited-edition Fox Trap case, or sponsor Running up the Stairs While Carrying Scissors contests in local bars.

Most Unfortunately Named Beer: Blatz. There is a rule

in beer marketing: never choose as your brand name a word that implies the consequences of beer drinking. Honorable Mention: Schlitz.

Best Beer for Those Who Enjoy Watching Golf on TV, but Find It Leaves Them Winded: the Schaefer Weekender, a twelve-pack ($2.99).

Best Mascot: the Hamm's Beer Bear. Slope-shouldered, dumb as a stump, with a gut so big it has calluses from where it hits the ground. Bartender? More Hamm's, please!

Let me conclude with my personal favorite: Rolling Rock, the official beer of the Trilateral Commission–Illuminati–Masonic Conspiracy. Each bottle has, for no apparent reason, the number "33" stamped on it somewhere. Even more odd, there's a rambling, stilted paragraph printed on each label —something about tendering this beer as a tribute to your good taste, etc. It reads like an anagram of something else —the name of Satan, perhaps. And guess what: *there are exactly 33 words in this message.* That's right—all those guys you see slouched over the bar, pulling sips from Rolling Rocks—they're all part of the international masonic conspiracy. Frightening how well they blend in, isn't it? And how *many* of them there are.

But beer is beer. Buy what you will, drink it in moderation, and be not ashamed that you didn't pay a day's wages for your beverage. Just avoid the ones with the Monk. And if you see a beer with a Monk on a Harley? Leave the store. Immediately.

The Rainbow Tribe

THERE WAS A NAKED MAN IN THE MIDDLE OF THE ROAD
playing a banjo. Actually, just holding a banjo. And not at
fig-leaf level, either. He grinned at all the passersby, as if to
say, "Hey! How about this! Naked, with a banjo!"

No one paid him much attention. This was, after all, the
Naked Banjo Holder's Convention. And the Friends of Bi-
sexual Dolphins Convention. The Wiccan Lesbians for the
Metric System Convention. The Fraternal Order of Stringy
Caucasian Males with No Marketable Skills. And a hundred
others. They are the Tribes of the Rainbow Nation, and this
was the Rainbow Gathering.

Once a year this loose and variegated group fills up a
national forest for a week, drawing its members from across
the country; this year they chose the Superior National Forest
in northeastern Minnesota. Over 5,000 celebrators joined the
Gathering this year, and I, much to my initial dismay, was
one of them. I've never put much stock in the hippie ethos.
A child of the '70s, I regarded the late '60s as a bad costume
drama, lazily written, ineptly performed. Tie-dyed shirts,
eye-searing incense, the interminable caterwauling of the
Grateful Dead, all that vague and gaseous peace-'n'-love

219

nonsense—none for me, thank you. I'll be over here in the twentieth century, if you need me.

So I went to the Gathering with a glum face, expecting to have my favorite preconceptions reinforced by 5,000 hapless volunteers. And what did I find? Incense, tie-dyed shirts, the Grateful Dead, peace-'n'-love.

The punch line, of course, is good 'n' trite: it was one of the best days of my life.

It is a four-and-a-half-hour drive to the Gathering. Rich and I spy signs of the Tribe en route: the occasional shaggy man at the rest stop wheedling gas money out of white-belted tourists; the odd car with out-of-state plates, and a bumper full of the holy writ: NO NUKES, DEAD HEAD ON BOARD. Thirty miles from Lutsen we come across an ancient bus that has gone off the road. A wrecker is pulling it out of the ditch, a dozen white Rastafarians looking on in complete disinterest, fingering their dreadlocks. Ten miles later, we pass a parking lot filled with highway patrol cars. They've pulled over a van, made the driver take everything out, spread it on the steaming asphalt. This apparently requires twelve patrol cars.

We check into our hotel, a woody lodge along a crescent of lakefront, and go to the café to fortify ourselves with coffee before heading into the Gathering. We strike up a conversation with a rather taut young gentleman named Jim Elverhoy, breeder of gun dogs and professional taxidermist.

"Rainbows? They're everywhere. Kinda weird people. There was one who got up at a town meeting a few days ago, said 'I am Zeus, the god of mythology. You may worship me.' " Elverhoy grimaces. "I heard he *stank,* too.

"In fact, a local reporter went up, to interview them? And she was standing there, talking to 'em, and she passed out. Went to the doctor, and he said it was probably a combination of the incense and the B.O., just made her pass out." Lethal B.O. Wonderful.

Elverhoy pauses, shrugs. "But I don't know. They're not

220

doing any harm. I'm going in tonight, just to see what it's all about."

Spoken like a true open-minded, gun-dog-raising taxidermist. He gives us directions to the Gathering and we drive off.

The Caribou Trail is a thin, paved line drawn on the face of the deep northern woods, five miles of careening pavement developing into gravel. We are alone on the road; the only others we see are the white Rastas sitting in the shade of their bus. One of them squats on the engine block, coaxing magic from the stalled machinery.

Suddenly we spy a man standing in the road, waving us into a parking area. Hundreds of cars line the road, mostly battered, tetanus-infested jalopies. A few new cars. We find a spot, grab our gear, and head back to await the bus to the Gathering. Twenty hot and dusty people sit waiting—hippies, a couple skinheads, a few standard-issue teens with heavy-metal T-shirts, and three tidily dressed men who look as though they'd heard there was good shopping to be done but are beginning to doubt the truth of that advice.

The bus arrives, disgorges a brace of thin, grimy men. We get aboard.

"Welcome home, people," says the driver. "Welcome home."

Oh, now, really. This wasn't home. It had no electrical outlets, and it damn sure wasn't cable-ready.

"I feel like a Freedom Rider on this bus," one earnest young man declaims.

"What a long, strange trip it's been," says his companion, quoting a Grateful Dead song the perpetually stoned use to describe anything longer than a walk across the room.

"Welcome *home*, brother!" the driver cries. He is, I now realize, Charon, the boatman who ferried souls across the river to Hell. Which, in this case, is Woodstock. I have a sudden smothering attack of claustrophobia and we get off the bus to take a ride with a forest ranger.

We ride in with Bob Burton, a genial, white-haired man

who handles public relations for the forest service. He'd handled a Gathering before, in Michigan; he knew these people, and regarded them with a benign appreciation that does not always accompany a uniform and a badge.

"Some people around here are worried," says Officer Bob, "because whenever you get a bunch of folks like these together, you're going to see a strange culture. You're going to see nudity. But they're all right. Relaxed. They know what they're doing, they're organized, and they've worked closely with us to make sure this worked." Organization: the way to John Law's heart.

He drops us off near a bus encampment, points the direction of the Gathering, and goes off to chat with some folks. They see him, smile, wave him over. We shoulder our bags and walk. It's a long road, lined with old buses, old cars. A woman stands in a metal basin, taking a bath; two men are crouched over a camp fire, calling fire out of the logs. Long hair, ragged clothes. These people handed back their membership cards in the mainstream society a long, long time ago.

The road bottoms out at a small bridge. A man stands at a wooden gate, lifts it without a word to let us pass. The road before us slopes up, slides into the forest. We step on the other side of the gate, and—

And something changes. I can't say any more than that, or explain it; I just know that, all of a sudden, we want to be wherever it is we're going.

It's a long hike to the Gathering, half an hour. We pass few people—a couple of guys hunched in the weeds, some robust folk striding down the road, halloing us in greeting, a young man who is clearly preoccupied by some wondrous, whizbang lightshow in his brainpan. We pass Disappearing Dave's Christian Kitchen: all are welcome. A box of cast-off clothes sits by the camp, with a sign: FREE STORE. Along a stream, a message written on a paper plate: BOIL ALL WATER 15 MINS. The road is pristine. There's no trash, not so much as a cigarette butt.

We walk along, listening. After a life in the city, you tend to judge a forest by what you don't hear—honking horns, screeching people, Dopplerized pop music from passing cars. You commend the forest for being nice and quiet, like a good child. But as we listened, we started to hear the language of this place—birds chattering in a hundred tongues, insects droning their timeless monody, wind playing the forest like it was a flute with a million stops.

So, yes, I was sufficiently woolly headed before I even got to the Gathering. Something about a long walk in good spirits calms you, even if the road seems longer and longer and longer. We came across a young man with Oriental eyes who said he'd been telling people that the Gathering was just a quarter-mile ahead, even though it was much farther; people felt better when they heard the words "quarter-mile," he said. He'd noticed other people had picked it up. Everything around here was now a quarter-mile from everything else.

"So how far is it?" I asked.

"A quarter-mile. *Really.*"

And so it was.

The first thing you see upon entering the camp is the Triangle, the public square of the Gathering. It's almost medieval; everything appears to have been racheted down a few centuries on the scale of civilization. Minstrels stroll along, tootling on wind instruments. A message board is thick with manifestos, news items, exhortations to consider ferns as a viable substitute to toilet paper. There is an anarchist's manifesto, written on birch bark.

Take another look, and it's a Third World city. People are squatting in the dust, waiting for unreliable transportation. Vendors are sitting on the roadside, selling crystals, face painting, jewelry. Naked children poke through the gravel for something interesting to put in their mouths. Dogs trot about, engrossed in this wonderful encyclopedia of smells. Numd men stand in the road, bearing banjos.

It's the nudity that is initially disconcerting, but pleasantly so. There are a dozen women in the square untrammeled by foundation apparel. My first reaction is to elbow Rich as hard as I can and shout out, "Hot jiggity Moses, they're *nekkid!*" But there's nothing erotic in this tableau; the twin truths of nudism—it's not sexual in character, and the people who are nude aren't exactly what your id requested, anyway—are at work here. Some of these people are naked. So what?

The rest of the Triangle is given over to services—a medical tent, a herbologist's tent, a massage tent where several folk are having their haunches grimly pummeled. An information booth stands off to the side, presided over by John Roadrunner.

"It's good," he says. "It's what it ought to be. You got people here for the people, others who come to just *be,* you know, in the woods. There's a guy groovin' on the mud." He points to a man covered in mud, grooving. "Our job here is to help people to find what they're looking for—a quiet place for meditation, a noisy place for being noisy. And after it's over, we stick around, and disappear anything that's still here."

The Rainbow people are insistent on that point: they do not leave messes. There's no point in getting together to celebrate Mother Nature if you leave her with a few more crow's feet. At the last Gathering, Roadrunner points out, the Rainbow people planted over 200 tree seedlings provided by the Forest Service.

As for how people find out where the Gathering will be, Roadrunner says they just do, somehow. They ask at the co-ops, hear about it in magazines. The process of deciding where to go is a little more structured: a "vision council" is convened at the Gathering, a feather is passed, and people who've been praying for guidance link arms and present their ideas.

"Done by consensus," says Roadrunner. "Has to be 100-percent agreement."

"He's telling it like it is," says a wiry, intense man standing nearby.

I'm sure he is. Roadrunner is vintage hobo, with charm, goodwill, and a little sagely cunning in his smile. Fifty years ago, he would have ridden the rails. These being modern times, however, he is skilled at networking. He asks for my card.

It's hard to describe a day at the Gathering, since you don't really do anything. You sit around, breathe deeply, talk to whomever Providence places next to you. After a while you stop thinking; you hear a great and slow metronome working away in the forest, and you silently hum along to its rhythm.

We spend the afternoon walking the main streets of the Gathering. There are few open common spaces—everyone is assembled along two paths that slither through the forest. You can spend your day walking these roads, hailing whomever you meet, pausing to talk. You have the lake for cool wet comfort, the Sacred Meadow at the end of the South Fork for meditation. Everywhere there is the rich smell of the deep green woods, flavored with patchouli oil.

It doesn't look like thousands of people are here. Half the citizenry have melted into the woods off the paths; small colored flags tied to branches on the path indicate their residence beyond. Some of the camps are annual fixtures at the Gathering and provide food for those without provisions. Taco Hilton is such a place—a makeshift kitchen presided over by a topless woman kneading bread, paps a-flapping. According to the menu, she's making "Grateful Bread." Brewhaha is a camp renowned for its coffee; Popcorn Palace serves just what you'd expect. You don't pay to eat. But you help out, somehow, and add to what you have.

It seems possible to show up naked, hungry, and thirsty, and walk away clothed and belching. Giving to others who have a need is done with unexpected ease. Rich, for example, was perpetually thirsty, a hard dry sponge. He didn't have a cup, which was required to get water from the taps or buckets. No matter. People offered canteens, turned away

225

to resume conversation when he took his draught, knowing he wouldn't drink it all.

People also gave something both easy and immensely difficult to lend: courtesy. Nearly everyone we passed on the trail said hello. Skinheads said hello. Rastas called us brothers. Bookish topless young women beamed and waved.

One young man in a pale pink shirt sat on the edge of the road, stopped us as we approached. "You must answer a riddle before you pass," he said. Fine.

"What is greater than God, more evil than the Devil? The rich man wants it; the poor man has it; if you eat it"—he leaned forward, eyes flashing—"you die."

Hmmm. Well, according to St. Anselm's Proof, God is greater than that which can be conceived. So in terms of human perception, nothing can be greater than God.

"Yeah! Yeah! Think about it!"

And nothing can be more evil than the Devil . . . and the rich man wants for nothing—okay, I got it.

He waves us on. "New riddle tomorrow."

Hours later, we returned to the Triangle to take the shuttle out. I dropped down in the grass, watching the dogs play; Rich spoke with a woman who'd given birth at the last Gathering. Her child, an unfortunately scrofulous tot named Rush, played in the gravel while her mother described her theories on teaching children to watch. She had poise, grace, good teeth, and a patrician face; as she described the ballet lessons she had as a child, I wondered about her background. Whether her parents approved her roaming the country. Whether anyone's parents approved.

Look hard and you can see the costs of this lifestyle. It's not that these folks won't get ahead in this world—that's irrelevant to them. It's not that they are without, say, basic medical services—all they need do is show up at a public hospital, and the hard gray father of the state will step in and take care. They'll eat, they'll find shelter, they'll survive. But there is something sad in this hardscrabble life—coffee always coming from a rusty pot, feet always dirty, cold stares from the townsfolk wherever you go. These people have set themselves outside of the mainstream, and they prefer it that way. But they rub up against a different world on a daily basis, and surely they must tire after a few years. It can't always be fun to be cold and hungry in Eden, staring across the road at the doors of the Mall.

I was hungry. I wanted that shuttle to come and take me back to the hotel, for steak and napkins and ice cubes. But the shuttle did not come. I'd fled it in horror before, and now I prayed for it to come. John Roadrunner, still on duty at the information booth, said it would come in twenty minutes—but "twenty minutes," I had learned, was the chronological equivalent of "a quarter-mile." Everything was twenty minutes from happening. The shadows were starting to get long. If we didn't leave now, we'd be here all night. We began to walk.

And walk and walk. I felt tenpenny nails drive into my shins after the first three miles. We walked back to the gate where we'd entered, walked up through Bus City. People were streaming into the Gathering now, hundreds of them, plodding toward the camp. We felt as though we were going the wrong way, walking toward a city under siege. We found a police car, produced press badges, and asked for a ride back to the parking lot. Not an option. No rides given. Had to stay and control traffic.

"See any drug use?" said one officer. We said, truthfully, that we hadn't. Our usefulness ended, we were dismissed.

"We'd probably have gotten a ride if we said we'd seen some," Rich groused.

A local in a van, delivering food to the Gathering, picked us up and returned us to our car. It took half an hour of tortuous negotiation to get out of the parking area—it was a narrow lane clogged with cars going in both directions. Imagine twin Orson Welleses trying to pass in the aisle of an airplane.

"Goodbye, brothers!" a man shouted as we pulled from the lot. We sped back to the hotel, waving at the cars heading in.

I wanted hot and cold running civilization.

I also wanted to go back to the Gathering.

I went down to the lakeshore before supper. It was twilight, the sky and water meeting along the spine of the horizon like two pages of a vast book. Gulls, thoughtfully provided by whatever casting agency is in charge of picturesque scenery, wheeled and argued above. I knelt down where the water had laved the stones smooth, and considered why I felt so good.

It's this, and it's simple. The people of the Rainbow Tribe accept you without question. People I'd never acknowledge on the street had smiled and waved at me, simply because I was there, shared the uniform of skin. All distinctions were meaningless: race, body type, religion, ideology—all were minor embellishments on the basic idea, different ways of painting the same house. I tried to tell myself that it wasn't that easy, it wasn't that simple, that experience said otherwise, but I couldn't convince myself. Their simple, hug-a-tree, love-your-brother world is not some amusing, Technicolor sideshow. Our world is, in a sense, a bad parody of theirs. I suddenly realized what I had to do.

Get a banjo, be naked.

No. What kind of world would this be if everyone was naked, playing the banjo. Live like the Rainbow Tribe, and little, I fear, would get done. And we need to be known as a civilization that did more than just clean up after ourselves. Someone had to invent the engine that brought the tribe to the Gathering, build the factories that stamped out the buses, design the polymers that make up the nylon that shelters them. No need for all to grin in the dust.

But everyone ought to go to a Gathering, learn just what it is we have in common, feel what it means to live without distinctions. As a man told me on the shore of the lake, membership here is automatic. Everyone belongs.

Welcome home, people. A new riddle tomorrow.